ABANDON ME

MEMOIRS

MELISSA FEBOS

BLOOMSBURY

NEW YORK · LONDON · OXFORD · NEW DELHI · SYDNEY

FOR MY CAPTAIN

Bloomsbury USA
An imprint of Bloomsbury Publishing Plc

1385 Broadway	50 Bedford Square
New York	London
NY 10018	WC1B 3DP
USA	UK

www.bloomsbury.com

BLOOMSBURY and the Diana logo are trademarks of Bloomsbury Publishing Plc

First published 2017
This paperback edition published 2018

Author's note: Many names and identifying characteristics have
been changed to protect the identities of characters herein. Time has
been compressed and dialogue approximated. The events are as true
to my memory as possible. Literary representation is unavoidably
reductive, and for that I am sorry. I had to leave out so much.

ISBN: HB: 978-1-63286-657-8
        PB: 978-1-63286-658-5
        ePub: 978-1-63286-659-2

LIBRARY OF CONGRESS CATALOGING-IN-PUBLICATION DATA

Names: Febos, Melissa, author.
Title: Abandon me : memoirs / Melissa Febos.
Description: New York : Bloomsbury USA, 2017. | Includes bibliographical references and index.
Identifiers: LCCN 2016011681 (print) | LCCN 2016025070 (ebook) |
ISBN 9781632866578 (hardback) | ISBN 9781632866592 (eBook)
Subjects: LCSH: Febos, Melissa—Family. | Febos, Melissa—Relations with women. | Febos,
Melissa—Psychology. | Women—Identity. | Authors, American—21st
century—Biography. | BISAC: BIOGRAPHY & AUTOBIOGRAPHY / Personal Memoirs.
Classification: LCC PS3606.E26 Z44 2017 (print) | LCC PS3606.E26 (ebook) |
DDC 818/.603 [B] —dc23
LC record available at https://lccn.loc.gov/2016011681.

4 6 8 10 9 7 5 3

Typeset by RefineCatch Limited, Bungay, Suffolk
Printed and bound in the U.S.A. by Sheridan, Chelsea, Michigan

To find out more about our authors and books visit www.bloomsbury.com.
Here you will find extracts, author interviews, details of forthcoming
events and the option to sign up for our newsletters.

Bloomsbury books may be purchased for business or promotional use.
For information on bulk purchases please contact Macmillan Corporate
and Premium Sales Department at specialmarkets@macmillan.com.

Named One of the Best Books of 2017 by:
*Esquire, Refinery29, BookRiot, Medium, Electric
Literature, The Brooklyn Rail, Vol. 1 Brooklyn,
Largehearted Boy, The Coil,* and *The Cut*

Finalist, Lambda Literary Award for
Lesbian Memoir/Biography

Finalist, Publishing Triangle's Judy Grahn
Award for Lesbian Nonfiction

More Praise for *Abandon Me*

"Anyone who has read Febos . . . knows that her work explores boundaries as deftly as it defies categorization. In this new collection of essays, she once again obliterates convention with her erotically charged and intellectually astute recollections of family, relationships and the search for identity." —*Esquire*, **"The Best Books of 2017"**

"No subject is off-limits to Febos. She authorizes her reader to be braver, to dig deeper into their own secrets and to research those secrets in history . . . In her close reading and recording of her own life, Febos universalizes the pain of waiting . . . With each new piece Febos bends time." —*The Rumpus*

"The sheer fearlessness of the narrative is captivating." —*The New Yorker*

"The beautiful and bleak are shown with glistening coherence . . . The interwoven essays of *Abandon Me* emphasize the necessarily constructed nature of life narratives. Misery, as Philip Larkin has it, 'deepens like a coastal shelf.' Yet Melissa Febos's essays, while testifying to the truth of that process, also highlight the possibility of redemption, of something else that's deepening: our understanding." —*The Times Literary Supplement*

"[*Abandon Me*] is both intensely intimate and wide-ranging, as she pulls together insights from sources as disparate as psychoanalyst Carl Jung, jazz singer Billie Holiday and an ancient alchemical text. Febos is voracious in her emotional cravings, but none is stronger than her desire to know and own herself. The hard-won ending (truly, a beginning) is exhilarating." —Dawn Raffel for *O Magazine*

"*Abandon Me* is a beautifully written journey through Febos' world." —*BuzzFeed*

"From heroin addiction to romantic infatuation, [*Abandon Me*] considers forces powerful enough to inspire utter devotion, and the way that posture can both destroy and redeem." —*The Atlantic*

"Febos's gifts as a writer seemingly increase with the types of subjects and themes that typically falter in the hands of many memoirists . . . Febos transports, but her lyricism is always grounded in the now, in the sweet music of loss." —*The Millions*

"*Abandon Me* doesn't have graphic, shocking scenes like Febos's first, instead she goes further into the messy vulnerable, human parts of herself . . . I devoured these pages. Curled up on my coral-colored couch, I sometimes looked up as if someone might catch me in the act of crawling into her mind and living there for a while. It felt like I was being folded into her prose." —Natassja Schiel for *The Millions*

"I've heard it said that memoir asks not what happened, but rather, what the f*^%* happened, and throughout *Abandon Me*, Febos returns again and again, in lush prose, to this question. It isn't the answer that's most compelling (answers seldom are). Rather, it's the invitation *Abandon Me* offers the reader: to board her own ship, to hold her breath, and to leap into a dark and lyrical sea." —Cameron Dezen Hammon for *Hunger Mountain*

"[Febos] has emerged as one of our most creative and most unflinching memoirists, essayists, and teachers." —*Los Angeles Review of Books*

"Searing and eye-opening at every turn . . . A must-read." —*The Huffington Post*, "**27 Nonfiction Books By Women Everyone Should Read This Year**"

"With ruthless honesty, Febos follows the ebbs and flows of the loves in her life, from father figures to lovers." —*Marie Claire*

"Her mastery over metaphor is astonishing . . . What might be mere navel-gazing for a less brilliant author is made powerfully universal here. Though the particulars are hers, just about anyone can relate to the feeling of a chasm opening up inside. Febos's awakening to her full identity, even its ugliness, is a powerful and redemptive epic." —**Publishers Weekly (starred review)**

"*Abandon Me* examines the many loves of her life—lovers as well as family—with her distinctive blend of lush language and relentless intelligence." —Jackie Thomas-Kennedy for **Publishers Weekly**

"It's easy to fall in love with Melissa Febos' gorgeous new memoir of short essays . . . Febos brings a relentless curiosity and startling intimacy to the page . . . With her careful observations and introspection, she transcends isolation and captures the boundless nature of human emotion. *Abandon Me* is a fierce exploration of love and obsession, but it is something else as well—the story of a woman who is unafraid to explore the harsh truths and choices that shape our lives." —*Lambda Literary*

"Erotic and dark, the book is a courageous exploration of love as the ultimate form of plenitude and annihilation. A lyrically visceral memoir of love and loss." —*Kirkus Reviews*

"*Abandon Me* is a sonorous collection of concentric essays . . . Febos' lyrical musings are intercut with astronomy, antiquity, and pop culture analyses—from *Ferdinand the Bull* to the musical fantasy film *Labyrinth* . . . Febos engages a process of self-discovery that confirms an exceptional skill at illuminating universal truths." —Megan Labrise for ***Kirkus Reviews***

"[A] raw, brave work about truly knowing oneself." —***Library Journal***

"[In this] collection of self-aware, stylish, autobiographical essays on love, addiction, and inheritance . . . Febos harnesses language, moods, actions, and settings with precision. A professor of creative writing, she stuns with sentences that are a credit to her craft and will no doubt inspire her readers." —***Booklist***

"Riveting . . . Emotionally raw and stirring in a way that will have you aching for more." —***Newsweek*, "Best New Books of the Week"**

"Febos is a talented writer with a colorful personal history." —***The Washington Post***

"Intimate and mesmerizingly vulnerable . . . Gets at the heart of who we love, how we love—and why." —***Refinery29*, "Our Favorite Books Of 2017"**

"[*Abandon Me*] circles back around different stories, weaving together an exploration of her origins with moments taken from [Febos's] childhood, addiction, recovery and her work as a dominatrix." —***The New York Times Book Review***

"A frequently stunning book, dealing with questions of family, identity, and intimacy." —*Vol. 1 Brooklyn*

"Febos has established herself as a gifted writer with deep reserves of empathy and a bottomless hunger for personal truth . . . Her prose is exciting and inviting because it feels both raw and lived in." —*Guernica*

"[A] gorgeous writer . . . [with] stunning gifts for meta-phor and raw emotional truths." —*Minneapolis Star Tribune*

"*Abandon Me* proves unequivocally that there must be room in the literary canon for the complexity of women's stories on erotic fixation and loss." —*Bitch* magazine

"After the age of irony and clever or snarky tweets, it is refreshing to see a work that is as earnest and heartfelt as *Abandon Me*. Even through this earnestness, Febos manages to add in a complexity and density that keeps the work interesting . . . After all, not every book ranges over as diverse topics as David Bowie, Borges, and Jungian analysis. These wide ranging interests help to make *Abandon Me* a lively, surprising, and distinctive book . . . Not to be missed." —*Kenyon Review*

"Fans of Febos' previous memoir, *Whip Smart*, will find *Abandon Me* a delicious follow-up to the salacious stories of her work as a dominatrix. Those new to her writing will be insatiable for more after digging into her new offering, which details the queer writer's relationship to love, loss and erotic addiction." —*GO Magazine*

"*Abandon Me* is an exploration of self-discovery. Febos's collection of memoirs explores not only the act of abandoning, but also different types of love and growing up . . . Febos meditates over the concept of abandonment quite like [Leslie] Jamison meditates on the idea of empathy . . . Febos sketches in staggering detail her adolescence of abandonment." —*Chicago Review of Books*

"Febos complicates the human desire for connection with explorations in philosophy, psychology, and accounts of historical repression that seduce readers into inhabiting her myths while resisting sentimentality by dismantling the fictions with deft intellectual probing reminiscent of the work of Maggie Nelson . . . One of Febos's greatest literary strengths is her ability to make these intimate experiences feel universal." —*BOMB Magazine*

"A fiercely intelligent and remarkably intimate essay collection about the border between love and obsession." —Leigh Stein for *The Rumpus*

"There is something pioneering about the way Melissa Febos talks about love, connecting it to all its binary shadows . . . This book as a treatise on the siren call that leads us to re-stage events that have wounded us, so that we can produce a different ending, is absolutely luminous. The writing is crisp and unsettling." —*KQED Arts*

"Lovely, very deep essays. It's raw and vulnerable; the writing is gorgeous ... Smart and surprising. If you like Maggie Nelson and Leslie Jamison, it will be right up your alley. I was very surprised and immediately gripped from the first page by the quality of her writing and by how open she is ... It's uncommon." —*Book Riot's All the Books* **podcast**

"Astonishing ... Febos's stirring prose—her delicately wrought sentences and stellar sense of pacing—don't distract from the narrative arcs themselves, which is a relief, as each braided essay carries a beginning, middle, and end." —***Book Riot*, "Best Books of 2017 So Far"**

"Finishing the book felt like lying in bed after sex with a new lover, hoping arms would close around me but not wanting to ask for it ... *Abandon Me* commands an attention you'd have to beg for to be returned ... As Febos writes, in explanation of this paradox, 'we are all the conquered and conquerors.' So then, if to be left by Febos's writing is not the greatest pleasure you've ever felt, then you've read her book wrong. And that is the worst kind of abandonment." —*Brooklyn Magazine*

"This unflinching, lyrical, and often crushing memoir about love and the need for connection is a must-read." —*The Advocate*

"Febos' writing is unflinching, and her willingness to delve into her darkest corners avoids becoming overwhelming only because she handles it with strength and delicacy. *Abandon*

Me finds the universal in her own story and taps into many people's fears, pushing the reader to question what they might abandon themselves to or let themselves abandon."
—***Paste Magazine***

"Ambitious . . . I can't wait to see what Febos writes next."
—***Numéro Cinq***

"Febos is a learned, lyrical writer, as well as an associative thinker . . . *Abandon Me* has much to recommend it: candor, a tone blessedly free of self-pity, and, for all those who ever flipped over the shiny side of love's bright coin and discovered dross, hope." —***Washington Independent Review of Books***

"The book explores shame, loss, and the meaning of family with such tenderness and vulnerability that readers can't help but look at their own wounds through a more empathetic and, hopefully, healing lens." —***Barnes & Noble Review***

"[Febos is] one of our most fearless and poignant writers . . . Here is a work that is both poetic and narrative, compassionate, raw and original. *Abandon Me* is a fiercely intelligent and remarkably intimate investigation of love and obsession, trauma and resiliency." —***The Brooklyn Rail***

"[Febos] is able to simply flay herself on the page while never alienating the reader and always making us feel like we somehow are included in her life's journey, even when we have nothing (or everything) in common with her . . . Mesmerizing and smart." **—Read It Forward, "Favorite Reads of February 2017"**

"Fiercely intelligent and intensely intimate . . . Here is a work poetic and narrative, compassionate, raw and original." **—The Writers' Block Blog**

"It defies easy description or categorization, and begs to be reread, to be unpeeled, layer after layer." **—Fiction Advocate**

"Striking and masterfully crafted." **—The Boiler**

"As brilliant and insightful as it is beautiful and entertaining." **—Rebellious Magazine**

"The essays build into an interrogation of relationships, idolization, and how the author's past intertwines with cultural history. Though the book explores bonds that Febos has with others—lovers, friends, lost and found family members—the relationship it ultimately depicts is the one that she builds with herself. It is also an origin story about creating the life of an activist, artist, teacher, and cultural theorist." **—Bookforum**

"[Febos] is a gorgeously lyrical and insightful writer . . . A recording and reckoning of love and loss and longing, evoked in gorgeous language dripping with sensuality, hope, and pain . . . We recognize our own losses in hers and understand them better through her wisdom and insight. We feel

relieved to see them so beautifully and viscerally rendered."
—*Ploughshares*

"A powerful, poignant meditation on not only the pain of loss but also the maddening, intoxicating, confusing, and exhilarating effects of true human closeness." —**Meghan Daum, author of *The Unspeakable***

"*Abandon Me* is a voluptuous book about the relationship between sex and surrender, desire and addiction, vulnerability and power. Febos unfolds her dark romance with erotic charge and sensuous poetry." —**Sarah Hepola, author of *Blackout***

"It's rare to read a book as generous as it is genius. Febos intimately explores addiction, pain, pleasure, the uncontrollable character, and the strangely joyful and terrifying nuances of abandonment. I don't know that I've ever felt more thankful to read a book. *Abandon Me* found me when I most needed it." —**Kiese Laymon, author of *How to Slowly Kill Yourself and Others in America***

"An intricately constructed and emotionally devastating book about the appearance and disappearance of love. Febos is a strikingly talented writer who pushes at the boundaries of her form and shows us just how amazing and expansive it can be." —**Jenny Offill, author of *Dept. of Speculation***

"Melissa Febos is the anthropologist and critic; the learned, dispassionate observer; and the passionate advocate of her body's passage through time, space, and the woes and pleasures of contact with other humans. *Abandon Me* reflects an extraordinary range of both experience and understanding." —**Vijay Seshadri, Pulitzer Prize–winning author of *3 Sections***

"Intellectual, erotic, and lyrical, this book arrives at emotional truths that startle and dazzle. Febos spares no one. And who would want to be spared such ravishing?" —**John D'Agata, editor of *The Making of the American Essay***

"Riveting and heartbreaking and tough and passionate and beautiful and original; a tour de force. Melissa Febos weaves the personal and the universal together into a provocative, brilliant, incredibly moving examination of power and identity." —**Kate Christensen, author of *Blue Plate Special***

"Melissa Febos is a deep, broad, and fearless thinker. This hard-fought, hard-won, endlessly compelling, and elegant memoir teaches us that our traumas are not isolated, but in constant conversation with each other, and promises that if we listen carefully to their steady murmuring, we might find the means and the power to heal our lives." —**Pam Houston, author of *Contents May Have Shifted***

"This book made me feel more than I was prepared to about desire and identity, as though it were an exquisite vivisection of what we politely call 'falling in love.' Febos's *Abandon Me* is extraordinarily written and unflinchingly bold." —**Nadia Bolz-Weber, author of** ***Accidental Saints***

"No one tells it like Melissa Febos. Sensual, lyrical, raw, brave, and honest, *Abandon Me* is simply gorgeous." —**Ann Hood, *NYT*-bestselling author of** ***The Knitting Circle*** **and** ***An Italian Wife***

Bookseller Praise for *Abandon Me*

"It is a rare and precious thing whenever I find a writer that makes me feel as heart-filled and glad to be a reader as how I felt when I read the prose of Melissa Febos. With emotional inklings of Maggie Nelson and Jenny Offill—and a heart-wrenching voice all her own—Febos's *Abandon Me* seduced and entranced me. I couldn't help but underline, dog-ear, and hover over every single page. An honest tale of the pains of love and loss, *Abandon Me* urges us to listen, to empathize, to desire without fear." —**Claire Tobin, Literati Bookstore, Ann Arbor, MI**

"A memoir like none other. Febos exposes the complications of identity, addiction, obsession, jealousy, forgiveness, trust, and abandonment—weaving into each scenario mythological, psychological, and literal interpretations. She forces you to evaluate your own stories and their power. How you abandon yourself to discover your true worth is the substance of Febos's powerfully honest memoir." —**Mindy Ostrow, River's End Bookstore, Oswego, NY**

"What is it about need and desire; the belief that some thing, some high, some person will save us or complete us, despite that very thing leading us further away from ourselves? Melissa explores these issues with pinpoint attention even while she's losing her edges. Ultimately it is the power of her focus and the grace of her writing that enables her and the reader to pull back and see the possibility of having a life more whole." —**Sheryl Cotleur, Copperfield's Books, Sebastopol, CA**

"Febos beautifully interprets her most intimate moments in order to make peace with what we all fear the most. This book compels its reader to reflect and to reach out." —**Gwen Corkill, Brookline Booksmith, Brookline, MA**

"Beautiful, expressive, and poetic. Anyone who has experienced the highs and lows of an intense romantic (and often unhealthy) attachment will identify with this memoir. But the truly special moments are when Febos is exploring her relationship with her father(s) or ruminating on favorite books, the beauty and nuance of language, philosophy, native culture, and the meaning of home." —**Adrian Newell, Warwick's, La Jolla, CA**

"It is amazing to read a memoir that is both so lyrical and raw. Febos reveals all of her scars and tender parts, allowing us to feel the depth of her pain and desire. A truly beautiful meditation on the complexity of love and resilience." —**Luisa Smith, Book Passage, Corte Madera, CA**

"Febos has the sense of structure of Rebecca Solnit and the accuracy in exploring sexuality of Maggie Nelson's *The Argonauts*. *Abandon Me* is for fans of beautiful creative nonfiction." —**Jesse Bartel, BookHampton, Southampton, NY**

"What is love and what makes it worth it? What is heritage and family, and how does that define us? In Melissa Febos's beautiful and heartbreaking memoir, she seeks to answer these most profound questions. I was completely captivated by this raw and, at times, brutally honest book." —**Julie Slavinsky, Warwick's, La Jolla, CA**

"A relentless examination of desire, loneliness, love, and reading. Melissa Febos displays a remarkable emotional honesty, one that exposes her life, but also, as in the best confessional memoirs, casts light on the reader as well." —**Stephen Sparks, Green Apple Books, San Francisco, CA**

"Febos's courage is astounding. I found resonance in her experience—and her craving to understand it all. Moreover, I relished the view into her passionate, uninhibited, and ever-so-slightly chaotic life. I took from it a comfort in my own—and a greater compassion for hers. It that sense, *Abandon Me* is an ideal memoir." —**Becky Dayton, Vermont Book Shop, Middlebury, VT**

CONTENTS

One does not become enlightened by imagining figures of light, but by making the darkness visible.

—Carl Jung

It is a joy to be hidden and a disaster not to be found.

—D. W. Winnicott

I have destroyed everything: our hands, our arms, our tangled hair, the silence, the night.

We parted, we waited for each other, we saw fear's chasm open between us. If the thread of our waiting should break, we shall fall into the bowels of the earth.

—Violette Leduc, *Thérèse and Isabelle*

No one can articulate a syllable which is not filled with tenderness and fear, which is not, in one of these languages, the powerful name of a god.

—Jorge Luis Borges, "The Library of Babel"

We had no television, no god, no family less than a day's drive away, but we had stories.

"Once upon a time in Spain," read my sea captain father, *"there was a little bull and his name was Ferdinand."* His back against the couch, me the fat baby on his chest, the curtain drifting over us as summer pushed through the open window. I mouthed every word he read, studied the shine of that cow mother's eyes, the curve of Ferdinand's eyelashes beneath the cork tree.

It was a storybookish early life—my beautiful mother and her curly-haired captain, our town surrounded on three sides by the ocean. Out my bedroom window glittered a lake of murky depths. In my bedroom, a trove of stories. We were lucky and we were loved, which isn't the same as happy, if you believe in such a thing.

Today, my beloved and I drove from her desert home to a nearby city for a conference. Now, in the hotel bed, we read Hemingway's *The Dangerous Summer*, in which he follows rival matadors Luis Miguel Dominguín and Antonio Ordóñez across Spain during the summer of 1959. The book is her selection—she has been to Spain, has seen a toreador lifted into the air by a horn in his thigh.

"It was a good day for bulls at Aranjuez on May thirtieth," she begins.

The first time I heard her voice, I sat in a room full of people. The dark was thick with heat. All of us listening. I carried a story of my own into that room, but her voice silenced everything in me. There was a pool of light and in it she gripped the podium's shoulders, *Listen to me*—and I did not remember myself until she let go.

"The river was brown and swollen from the rains," she continues. Cheek to her chest, I listen to more than the story. Her skin's smell—salted honey, the smooth and muscle of our pressed thighs, the lull of sleep and our slowed pulses. They become one. Just as the desert and the sky's hundred-houred layers of color and the mountains and the dry tongue of road and the dead rattlesnake we found in it this morning—scaly rope fat enough to dock a boat—and the wide open parts of my chest become one. Enormous.

When the Captain was home from sea, he woke from nightmares, screaming. When he was gone, my brother and I did. We counted time in waves. My brother suffered terrible nightmares. I became a sleepwalker. In the silent hours, I rose from my bed, pajamas soaked with sweat. I walked the halls and climbed the furniture. I searched the empty spaces of our house. I haunted his side of my parents' bed, opened cupboards and closets, boxes and drawers. My mother found me moonlit, straddling the back of the couch, staring out the window. Six years old and already a widow walker. She led me back to bed. In the morning, I woke salt-white.

When I didn't sleepwalk, I counted all the dangers my father might meet: storms that turned the sea foaming, fanged, ravening for ships; two-hundred-ton beasts big enough to gulp a school bus, gulp my captain, our Jonah. And if so, what then? What god would compel the Captain coughed up onto the shore, to leave the sea for good? He didn't believe in any god. He didn't want to come home.

I knew that pirates always kill the captain first. They slit his throat to show the crew they are not afraid to bloody the decks. The moonlight trapped my fears in its shadows, played them against the walls of my bedroom. The Captain had met such storms, had even fought such pirates. Didn't real heroes eventually run out of happy endings?

When he was at sea, I never cried. My brother and I never spoke of missing him. We crawled out from nightmares and into my mother's bed. *Read,* I'd say. My mother never stuttered when she read, and never wept, and when my mother read, I believed her. Whether we knew what came next or not, we trusted those stories because we could not trust our own.

Once upon a time, after one kiss and a month of letters, I flew across the country to meet an almost stranger, my future beloved. We spent two days together: all body, few words. But on the last night—before I left, before we knew when next we'd meet or as what—she got a call that her mother was ill.

What's wrong? I asked. At first, she would not or could not tell me. When she did, I said nothing. I had dreaded such a call all my life. I knew better than to tell her it would be okay. It might not have been. It is hard enough to accept comfort from those who know us and nearly impossible from those who don't. *Can I read to you?* I finally asked. It was the only comfort I knew well enough to offer. *Rilke?* I asked, because I'd brought *The Book of Hours* in my suitcase.

No, she said. It requires so much trust to accept another's solution. We did not have enough.

The Book of Hours is a book of love poems to God, though Rilke was in love with a married woman when he wrote them. So, I think it must also be a book about loving a woman. Maybe every desire is the desire to give ourselves away to some perfect keeper, to be known perfectly, as only a creator could know us. So many of the lines in his "Love Poems to God" are the promises we want from our lovers. Maybe *The Book of Hours* is about how love makes women into gods. Not the kind we seek in churches, but the Greek kind—the kind whom to love might scorch the human lover dead, or turn her into a different kind of animal. The kind we create, who are too human in their loving us.

Like Rilke, I had fallen in love with a married woman. Across those 2,500 miles, she began the slow process of prying her life apart. Soon after our first weekend together, I sent her some of Rilke's lines: "Let everything happen to you: beauty and terror / Just keep going. No feeling is final / Don't let yourself lose me." I wanted to be strong for her, but it was already hard to see a happy ending across all those miles. I waited, as I had waited all my childhood, though it never got easier.

I can't do this, I whispered to myself in the morning shower.

I can't do this, I heard in love songs on the radio as I drove to work.

I can't do this, I told my friends after her wife called me on the phone.

I can do this, I said into her hands, and then pressed that promise against my body, as if her touch could make it true.

Uncertainty and distance are similar afflictions—even more irreconcilable problems than an incumbent wife. The mind—dumb, houndish thing—still tries to solve them. I was tireless and so tired. I became forgetful. I grew thin. I grew angry. *Where are you?* I kept asking, but she had no answers. I had to wait.

Rilke, my beloved later told me, pushed his wife down the stairs. Or so she had heard. *Yes*, I thought, *love can kill you, after all. Yes*, I think now, *love can be that selfish*. It is hard to care rightly for someone you fear losing. It becomes possible to also hate them.

When the Captain no longer came home to our house, but to a house in another part of town, my mother traded her tears for psychotherapy textbooks. From them, we learned how to name our feelings. *Are you angry?* my mother asked us. *How about sad?* I shook my head. My brother refused to sleep.

In my twenties, in New York, my friends and I made punch lines of our abandonment issues. And in certain moments, in our therapists' offices, we could glimpse their true size, like the dark length of a whale passing beneath a boat. It stole my breath—the shock of my own smallness, the strength of the unseen, how easy capsizing could be.

Abandonment. What did that really mean? That I was left? That I had learned to leave my self. That I would retell the story until I found a different ending. Until I learned to stay.

Rilke took his title from the book of hours, a popular Christian devotional text of the Middle Ages. At the university where I teach, the library's special collection houses remnants of these prayer books. The oldest is from 1420 France. One afternoon, sick with longing, I washed my hands and sat at the long wooden table in that cloistered room and laid them out around me.

The first books in creation were inked by hand on animal skins, and sitting with these pages under those soft lights, their textures—delicate as sloughed sheaths of faith—were enough to convince me that books were once bodies, that the bestial and the divine can reside in the same place.

Fruit-laden vines bordered some pages, so precisely rendered that they still crept across those milky margins, blushing with pinks and reds six centuries faded. I squinted at the careful calligraphy inside, each letter drawn by the same slow hand—words opening like black buds across the leaves.

Books of hours were among the first books possessed by women, and sometimes the prayers inside even held the name of the book's owner. I traced those gold edges, the monogram engraved on a cover. How had it felt to touch these first pages? To carry these holy words home and read your name among them? Like being found, I thought.

I had always searched for myself in stories, and Pippi Longstocking was a likely candidate. The nine-year-old daughter of a sea captain, she lived alone with her monkey and her horse, and repaired her own home when necessary. Pippi's self-sufficiency was written as freedom. Pippi had spent years aboard her father's ship and brimmed with tales of their adventures. Though her father had been lost at sea, she spun stories of his being made the king of a savage isle.

These ought to have been my favorite stories. But Pippi held no special fascination for me, the actual nine-year-old daughter of a sea captain. Shouldn't I have wanted super-human strength? To need no one? To accompany the Captain on his seafaring adventures? Of course I did. But I knew better.

That child reader wanted, as this writer does, to find my troubles on the page, and then, hopefully, to see them resolved. Pippi's problems were already solved. If her self-sufficiency were hard won, it happened off the page. And she was a fool—I knew her father was dead.

While my brother memorized stories of boy warriors—Hiawatha and Peter Pan—I preferred *The Velveteen Rabbit*, whose hero believes that love has made him Real, until he meets a living rabbit. O, the pain of discovering that a thing is not what you thought it was! Worst of all, to discover this about yourself. When his boy contracts scarlet fever, the rabbit is stuffed into a sack of things to be burned.

My heart broke with the rabbit's. To be found unlovable was a kind of death—the child's animal wisdom knows they are tantamount. The rabbit's despair is so great that he cries a real tear, summoning the nursery fairy, who finally makes him Real.

The nursery fairy is a *deus ex machina*—she pops out of a flower to perform her magical solution and is nowhere else mentioned in the story—but that never bothered me. The rabbit's pains were real. Like him, I wanted to be loved. Like him, I feared being found unworthy. What if the Captain's absence was proof of this? In a terrifying wordless place, I harbored a suspicion that it proved I was not Real.

When I learned to read, I read: to myself, to my menagerie of stuffed animals, to my little brother. I started with the familiar ones, the stories in which my parents' voices first comforted me. Soon, the comfort of my own reading voice replaced theirs.

Even without an audience, I read—the silent words vibrating my skull, filling the places where grief might have settled. I spent so many waking hours in stories that when I lifted my gaze the rooms of our house blurred, furniture and faces floating by me detached from context, like characters in a film whose plot I'd half forgotten.

I was both looking for and leaving myself. Now, I remember the rabbit's sadness better than my own. Memory renders the gray desolation of the moors in *The Secret Garden* more precisely than the sad New England sea of my own girlhood. Only by exiling my own grief to those foggy plains could I find and face it.

I had learned to wait for the Captain and feel nothing. This was different. Nine months in love with this woman, I waited: at baggage claim in the airport, for her to call me back, to end her marriage, to promise me that she would be there. There was no distraction. I could not read. I could not write. I could not sleep. I cried bottomless, ugly cries that no lover should see. It was a despair so furious that a friend and I named it "Bertha," after the mad wife of *Jane Eyre*'s Mr. Rochester. My grief was a madwoman who had been locked for years in the attic. Finally freed, she set fires. She was an animal. She would not be locked away again. *My therapist tells me to love her*, I said. *But I think I need to kill her*.

After ten months, my beloved said, *enough*. She said, *I can't do this anymore*. She left and I could not stop her. I did not sleepwalk or search my night-swept house. She was not lost at sea, but she was lost to me. I had no story to make sense of it.

The Captain doesn't remember my abuela ever reading to him, though she claimed she did. *And I have a really good memory*, he says in a small voice.

He was the middle of three sons. He was the altar boy, the one who carried a crumpled brown paper bag of toy soldiers everywhere. In the midst of any chaos, he could sit himself in a corner, open that bag, and disappear into the world of those plastic men. It was a lucky power, as my abuelo was a mean drunk. He tossed my abuela around their house like one of her religious figurines. Sometimes, she broke. Every morning, she said her prayers. She hid her bruises. She dressed her boys for school. My abuelo did not stop beating her until the day her middle son grew big enough to stop him. *If you ever hurt her again,* he said, *I'll kill you.*

The Captain needed stories, the sense they might have made of that life. At their best, that is what children's stories do: force logic upon the gruesome facts of our lives. They mirror our troubles and submit them to a chain of causality. The heroes of children's stories suffer, but for reward—even if their happy ending is only the restoration of order. Rumpelstiltskin's queen keeps her first-born child. Hansel and Gretel kill the witch. The Velveteen Rabbit is made Real. Better still, the oldest stories written for children often offer retribution. In Grimm's original, Rumpelstiltskin is so enraged at having lost that he tears his own body in half. Cinderella's evil stepsisters cut off their feet, and doves peck out their eyes.

Who knows what plots the young Captain built, row by row, for those miniature men. Maybe there was no story that could have made sense of that horror.

The Captain could not speak of my missing him, could not name or make sense of it. But many of my earliest memories are of his reading to me. His favorite was *The Story of Ferdinand*, and when I look at the drawings of that little bull under his cork tree, I understand why. Like Ferdinand, he was no fighter. The men from Madrid forced Ferdinand into the ring, and so a man forced my Captain. But when Ferdinand refused to fight, he was taken home. The Captain never had that choice; his home was the ring. And the story that saved him was the sea.

My mother's favorite story was C. S. Lewis's *The Voyage of the Dawn Treader*. In volume five of the *Chronicles of Narnia*, Lewis transports the Pevensie children from a subway in London to the ship of Prince Caspian, with whom they voyage to the eastern edge of the world.

My mother's captain, her prince, was gone. She waited and waited for him. Eventually she left him, but leaving was never what she wanted. Maybe, if he had asked, my mother would have boarded that ship. If she could not be his greatest adventure, she'd have settled for sharing it.

Our favorite stories can be like lovers. Make sense to me, we ask them. Make sense *of* me. Here, fix these hurting parts. And stories do, sometimes better than our lovers.

When my beloved came back to me, nothing was easy. *How could you leave me?* I asked her again and again. There was no right answer. There was no way to prove that she would not leave again. She grew weary of trying. I grew weary of waiting. I began to understand how a woman could leave the captain she loved.

Jorge Luis Borges wrote that "To be in love is to create a religion whose god is fallible." Of course I was still wanting; love had not made me Real, which is to say it had not made me safe. I had believed in something perfect, and it had capsized me. In his *Book of Hours*, Rilke says, "To each of us you reveal yourself differently: to the ship as a coastline, to the shore as a ship." That is, love doesn't give us a god, unless we are also willing to become one.

Fighting did not fix us. No amount of talking seemed to help. Finally, in a moment close to hopeless, I asked, *Can we read?*

One of the first stories we read was Borges's "The Library of Babel," in which he depicts the universe as an infinite library. As I curled against her, my pulse slowed. In my beloved's voice, Borges lamented "man, the imperfect librarian." Reminded me that "the universe, with its elegant endowment of shelves and enigmatical volumes, of inexhaustible stairways . . . can only be the work of a god." That though its pages may sometimes appear to me "a mere labyrinth of letters," I am not meant to comprehend them. There were forces greater than that of my lover, than that of my longing. I did not have to be certain to believe in something.

Over the phone, through the computer, into the pixelated darkness of each other's bedrooms, we began reading each other to sleep.

"*Call me Ishmael,*" I said. "*Consider the subtleness of the sea; how its most dreaded creatures glide under water.*"

"*It is not down on any map,*" she answered. "*True places never are.*"

Melville gave us answers. Lorca, the words we did not have.

"*My head is full of fire,*" I told her, "*mi casa es ya mi casa.*"

"*If I told you the whole story it would never end,*" she explained. "*But I found / the hemlock-brimming valley of your heart.*"

The Story of Ferdinand was published in 1936, on the cusp of the Spanish Civil War, and the tale's pacifist message provoked divisive reactions. Hitler ordered it burned. Gandhi named it his favorite book. Ernest Hemingway, that most pious patron of bullfights, was so offended that he penned a rebuttal story, "The Faithful Bull." Unlike Ferdinand, Hemingway's bull lived to fight, "and he would fight with deadly seriousness exactly as some people eat or read or go to church."

Like that of Ferdinand, Hemingway's story ends with its hero in his glory. Rather than under a cork tree, the Faithful Bull meets his end in the ring. Ironically, Hemingway's closing line, "Perhaps we should all be faithful," could have as easily closed *The Story of Ferdinand*. Both made the same point: an animal has its nature, and faith to that nature is righteous. They do not promise ease nor redemption. To the faithful, to those who heed their own selves, both stories carry only the promise of being recognized for whom you are and taken home.

I do not know if my beloved can be a home to me, but I suspect that our story will reveal my own true nature.

Do you want to read tonight? became our refrain. Meaning, *I want comfort, the things that pain me cannot be spoken yet. They will not be soothed by speaking.* So we borrow words we can trust.

Any book could be our book of hours, though it makes sense that we now read Hemingway's *The Dangerous Summer*, because in our first year of love we had two dangerous summers. Because we recognize the worship and violence therein as our own. Hemingway's bullfight is not only a fight—it is a dance, a song, a kind of love—professed as only one body can to another. And every night, we build his story the same way, as we have built our own story: out of breath, from the shapes our mouths make, with the soft hammer of pulse.

Read, she tells me. We are in the hotel bed, but "Ernesto" is in Barcelona, and Antonio Ordóñez is in the ring. His rival, Luis Miguel, has done work with the muleta, "close enough to give the feeling of the nearness of tragedy within the marvelous security." The crowd has gone wild for him, but we know he is no match for Antonio, not in Ernesto's eyes.

My beloved presses her lips to my head as I read and moves her fingers, lithe banderillas, across my chest. I lean my face into her and she nudges me back to the book. *Read*, she repeats.

The Dangerous Summer billows with words like *marvelous, perfection, beautiful, magnificent*. We laugh at Ernesto's infatuation with Antonio and the homoerotic depictions of the fights—his hero driving into the "death hole" over and over again. We laugh at the mentions of his wife, Mary, who appears only to announce an injured toe or a sunburn.

This, Hemingway's final work, was written as he slid into alcoholic death. Perhaps that explains all the perfections of his matador. Maybe they are the sentimental fixation of a drunk, dying man. Otherwise, perfection is only ever found in God and in love. Hemingway makes Antonio a god and perhaps he also loved him.

"Close enough to give the feeling of the nearness of tragedy within the marvelous security" is not Hemingway's best. It is, however, more accurate a description of our early love than any I have written. We are not unique in this. Still, it is hard to believe that anyone has ever felt such tragedy and security as that in my beloved's hand when she touches me. Maybe this kind of love always carries with it a fear of abandonment—that blade of fear, that wound of our past.

Antonio's first bull in Barcelona is a good one. The matador swings his muleta, "with delicate, calculated slowness just ahead of the bull's speed." She slides her hand down my belly and presses inside my thigh, pulls it open. Antonio circles, riling the bull, and "moving always into him," as her fingers move over me, lightly, then less lightly. I go quiet. *Read*, she says.

The bull's eye never leaves the muleta's red flash. His burning haunches shine, chest heaving with furious breath, but Antonio never hurries. He molds the bull, "instructing him, and finally making him like it and cooperate."

Sweat gathers where my lover's forearm crosses my hip, flexing with the motion of her hand on me. The crowd's noise swells at each pass as the corrida builds its conclusion, and she dips her mouth into mine. We both make a sound. Then she pulls away. *Read*.

Antonio, then, is "doing it all to music and keeping it as pure as mathematics and as warm, as exciting and as stirring as love." It is an impossible faena and he is doing it. He drives the sword in perfectly and I know and Hemingway knows and all the crowd knows that he loves the bull.

The book falls. She does not tell me to read. She tells me, *Come for me*. And I do. There are no more words. I am the rushing animal she has made me: all marvel, all mathematical magic, and music. I am perfect.

My first Christmas in the desert, just before bed, she gave me a slim, wrapped gift. I tore the paper to reveal a familiar book cover—red with white flowers. *The Story of Ferdinand.*

Read to me, she asked.

Once upon a time, I began, and told her of the little bull who did not want to fight. Before I was halfway through, she fell asleep. I kept reading. Listening to her steady breath, I stared at Ferdinand alone in that ring and felt the familiar ache of my own heart. It isn't gone. We find ways to comfort one another, and to comfort ourselves. And comfort eases, but it does not erase.

Until then, we keep reading.

LEAVE MARKS

We first made love in a hotel room in Santa Fe, where the five o'clock sun simmered on the horizon, grazing her shoulders with its fire as she knelt over my body. I watched her mouth open on my hipbone and leave a wet print that shone in the light as she looked up at me.

I had never been a lover who watched, but I watched her—hands tucked under my back as she bit my ribs, my belly, my breast. As her fingers slid inside me, her mouth latched onto my chest—the blank space just below my clavicle. I stopped watching then, stopped thinking of anything but the drive of her long fingers—how they filled me even as her mouth pulled, unraveling.

After, in the bathroom mirror, flushed and swollen, I leaned in and examined the purple splotch shaped like Rorschach's *card VI*, the most condensed inkblot of his ten. It is known as "the sex card."

It's embarrassing, I said, after I'd climbed back onto the bed beside her. *But I love hickeys.*

She laughed and slid her hand down my chest,

pressed the mark like a button with her fingertip. *You are wild.*

It'll fade by Monday. I smiled. My pleasure notwithstanding, to arrive on the college campus where I taught emblazoned with love bites was unthinkable. Even as defiant teenagers, we massaged them with frozen spoons, scrubbed them with dry toothbrushes, held icepacks to our necks as if to cool our racing pulses.

I'm writing an essay about hickeys, I told a friend.

Ew, she said and crumpled her face. Curious, I thought. We don't blink at sex as commerce—women's bodies propped across billboards and television screens, the familiar iconography of male lust. We coo at pregnant bellies, sanctify that most blatant acknowledgement of sex, but shame this ephemeral evidence. A hickey is personal. It offers nothing to its witness but recognition. Is our puritan history so strong in us that to acknowledge touch for pleasure's sake is vulgar? Maybe the hickey reveals other things, parts of our desire we'd rather not see in the light.

One family vacation when I was eight, I played in the pool with a halved rubber ball. Turned inside out, it would fling into the air with a satisfying *pop*. Somehow, I managed to suction this apparatus to the center of my forehead.

Look! I crowed to my poolside parents. And then, *Ow!* when it popped off of my face and splashed into the water. I rubbed my stinging forehead. When I looked up, my parents dissolved in laughter.

Oh, honey, my mother grinned. *Look what you did.* The rubber hemisphere had left a circular crimson bruise in the center of my forehead.

You've got a hickey on your face, said my dad.

What's a hickey? I asked.

Well, my mother said. *Sometimes teenagers like to suck on each other's necks until they get bruises, like the one on your forehead.*

I gaped, incredulous. *Why would anyone want to do that?* But later, in the hotel bathroom, when I looked in the mirror, I touched the dark mark so gently, leaned in to see it closer in repulsion, in wonder.

At ten, I discovered my neck. It felt like a secret my body had finally told me. A first drink, a light switch, a doorway where a wall had always been. Tracey Barren's mouth tore a hole in the hull between my shoulder and jaw, and water rushed in. That pleasure was a revelation: If this, then what?

After baseball practice, on a stray couch cushion in my basement, under an old beach towel, Tracey and I played "Date." She was always the boy. Her mouth on my neck. The sounds of my mother starting dinner upstairs. *Don't stop*, I said, for the first time.

From the start, our love had edges, the kind I can't help but touch—run my fingers along the jagged parts until they cut. For the first year of our relationship, my lover lived with another woman. She lived 2,500 miles away. When I saw her, after weeks of wondering, I was so hungry. I was angry. I was vibrating with fear. My mouth itched to close on her. As if that could make her stay.

Tenderness toward the object of our desire becomes an expression of love partly, I think, because it so defies the nature of want, whose instinct is often less to cuddle than to crush. My want was more gnash than kiss, more eat than embrace. I cared for my lover, but that kind of desire precludes many kinds of love. Hunger is selfish. I wanted her happiness. I also wanted to unzip my body and pull her into it, or crawl into hers. It is no accident that we go to the pulse. Lust is an urge to consume and perhaps there is no true expression of it that does not imply destruction. I can't say. But even my tenderness for kittens includes an impulse to put them in my mouth.

The sound of sucking means many things and all of them are synonymous with hunger. It is no wonder, our obsession with vampires, werewolves, flesh-eating zombies. Lust is also a desire to *be* consumed. The vampire's victim is arched in terrified ecstasy. We agree on this fantasy by the billion: devour us, leave us no choice but to surrender. Under my mouth, my beloved squirmed. Her hips rose, shoulders clenched, body resisted and yielded at once. The vampire is all measure and seduction until he tastes and loses control in the ravening.

One day, she held up a photograph in a magazine: a red fox, pointed face, yellow eyes embering.

Look, she said. *Like you. So little, so pretty, and so wild.*

Under this light I both preened and cringed. Like the bite marks on her neck, it revealed the animal in me who so often won.

Like no lover before her, she had seen these parts of me. Maybe she brought them out—how I get too hungry, eat too fast, chew with my mouth open. Jealousy heaves my chest and heats my hands, which sweat so often, those swift conductors of all feeling—both emotive and environmental. My teeth chatter easily though in sleep my temperature soars, a furnace metabolizing all the day's suppressed impulses. I felt embarrassed on the mornings we both woke smelling of my metallic sweat, as if I had revealed some grotesque secret.

My body has always given me away. Or maybe it's the other way around.

There is charisma in wildness and it was part of what drew her to me. How much I felt and how fast I moved. But so often the things that attract us are the things we grow to fear most. The things we want to change or control or keep only for ourselves. She began to instruct me. *Speak more softly*, she said. *Don't let them stand so close to you. You are mine*, she said, and oh, how I wanted to be hers. The opportunity to prove myself compelled me. It was not the first time.

Amelia, my best friend in fifth grade, must have been queer. Now, it's easy to armchair-diagnose her, to see how she fit my future type: razor-smart, broody with repressed anger, funny as fuck. Back then, I only knew the curious mix of fear and affection I felt for her. Like many vulnerable people, she defended herself with violence. Indian sunburns, pinches, and monkey bites—in which she clamped my skin between her knuckles and twisted—Amelia flowered my thighs and arms with bruises. Every time she moved, I flinched. It didn't stop me from spending every weekend at her house, though. That would have broken her heart.

I could see her tenderness, her lack of control, the fear that drove her to hurt me, and I could take the pain. It felt like a responsibility. It felt like a way to love her. Though it wasn't only for her.

I am a woman who likes to be marked and to mark. And I did then, too. There was a satisfaction in those bruises, in being the object of her reaching, in withstanding it. Sometimes, at eleven years old, I felt invisible, like a ghost haunting my own life. And the marks she made on me were a kind of proof. Like the ghost detected by glass she holds or the reflection in a mirror, Amelia's marks made me real. So many ways of being are intangible, can be explained away. Physical evidence is the easiest accounted. The things that mark us are the things that make us.

It isn't just me. Attachment and availability have been inscribed on human bodies for centuries, across continents. The Mursi people of Ethiopia insert lip plates in their girls as preparation for marriage, while the Kayapo of the Amazon use scarification and body painting. Contemporary North Americans are no exception; as we love to jab our flag into the earth, we brand our cattle, we mark our beloveds with bruises, babies, scars, disease, lipstick, and diamond rings.

My hickeys, too, are not simply an expression of desire, but also of ownership. During that first year, when my beloved lived with another woman, near the end of our visits

I would buckshot her neck, shoulders, and chest with hickeys. At least for the duration of those bruises, I could claim her body mine alone. I have always wanted to carve my name into the things I am afraid of losing. Perhaps the desire to leave marks is more honestly a desire not to be left.

And as much as we like to own, we also like to be owned in love. Or at least, to belong to someone. I am a feminist, and the desire to be possessed is one I have been reluctant to admit. I may not want to flash a diamond ring or replace my name with someone else's, but the mark of her mouth on me meant something similar—if not owned, then wanted. And who does not want to be wanted?

I developed early. By the time most of my classmates reached puberty, I was already a C-cup. As a result, my first kisses provoked a reaction that my less-developed peers did not suffer. Today we call it "slut shaming." And it happened to me before I even had a chance to be promiscuous.

Much as we worship them, we also like to punish promis-cuous women—or those whose sexuality is simply too evident. Sex is a slippery currency in a sexist society; access to my body worked in those boys' favor but against mine.

For a year I suffered sneers and crude gestures in the junior high school cafeteria. Prank calls to my family's home announced my sullied reputation. More than once I was groped in the school hallways. I absorbed that punishment without scrutiny and the shame of both my desires and my body was not easily unlearned. My brazenness as an adult who is unafraid to bear the evidence of her sex is partly restitution for those years.

There are other reasons why love bites are the domain of teenagers. For one, amateurism—the first hickey is often a mistake, and one that many never make again. In repeat offenses, there enters an element of braggadocio. The guy who breaks the bed and mistakes it for the best sex ever. *Look at us*, the splotch-necked teens gloat, *we are wild, we have sex*. Despite its glorification, sex is most novel to its initiates. The hickeyed teens are broadcasting old news to the rest of us—their entry into a club whose membership is public.

But my lover and I shared that novelty. While she lived with that other woman, and during the slow process of their separation, our public appearance as a couple was limited. I'd never had to hide my affections as an adult and that invisibility, however sensible, stung. I hated feeling like a secret and it spurred many fights between us. But much experience—not least mine as a former professional dominatrix—has taught me that restriction is the quickest route to fetishization.

After we were free to expose our desire, we did so with intention, in compensation for that year of hiding. I gave readings with my neck tattooed by her mouth. We posted pictures online of our bare midriffs pressed together. I'd never been so public a couple, and I wore it the way I had rainbow "freedom rings" as a teenager—giddy with visibility.

I read now about adolescents sucking on more obvious parts of each other in group activities that seem to preclude the secrecy and innocence of my own unsayable awakening. I don't so much mourn their lost childhoods. I lost mine at first opportunity and sex isn't the only way to do that. But I do remember the vacancy of those earliest and most obvious sex acts. I met desire under that faded beach towel, to the sound of cleats knocking the cement basement floor. What I mean is, the neck is always innocent. The parts of us we cannot see are touched most deeply, are most needing to be seen.

However insistent or ravenous the hickey, it is by nature temporary. There a time when my beloved and I considered getting matching tattoos on our ring fingers. We spent hours laboring over meaningful designs. For months I made appointments that she canceled at the last minute. She resisted that permanent mark for the same reason that I wanted it. Despite our mutual obsession, we did not trust each other.

Another year later, she revived the idea. As we drove past desert tattoo shops, she'd point. *Let's do it*, she'd say. *Why not?*

I'd nod, but never pull over. I had already stopped believing in the power of such symbols to make anything permanent. I had already stopped wearing her hickeys.

They say that passion wanes, that trust grows in its place. But after two years together, she and I still grabbed at each other like animals, like people who might never taste that particular salt again. Our passion never guttered. I kept waiting for trust to grow. The only thing to count on was our hunger, and the ways our bodies fed it. No mark of passion can make a love stay. It can only prove that it was.

I know the impossibility of the hickey, whose urge is not ultimately to mark or be marked, but to possess and be possessed. I cannot render anything precisely in words, as I cannot crush my lover's body inside of mine. All I can do is leave a mark—the notation of my effort, a symbol for the thing. That is the endless pleasure and frustration of the writer and the lover: to reach and reach and never become.

I could not make her mine any more than she could make me hers. The best I could do was to show her how much I wanted it. To press my mouth against her pulse, and open.

When I was seven, my sea captain father at sea, my mother a strobing lighthouse of missing, I stood alone in my bedroom, renaming all my toys Melissa. *You, and you, and you.* A child's narcissism, maybe. A punishment for my dolls. I didn't choose my name, but I could choose to give it away. A small triumph. But no matter how many dolls I christened Melissa, the sound of my name still shocked me: hum of M, soft L, hiss ending openmouthed. *Melissa*, my teacher called each morning. *Here*, I flinched.

It was a ribbon of sound, a yielding sibilant thing. Drag it along a scissor blade and it curls. I wanted a box, something with corners I could feel. Zoe or Katrina. Those girls ruled the school bus. You could press your fingers into Melissa. It was hum and ah, and esssss—more sigh than spit.

On family vacation in Florida, after days pickling in the hotel pool, eyes pinked from its blue brine, my mother asked me, *Melissa, why*, when the ocean was steps away, *why the pool?* Because the pool has sides, I told her. I was already spilling out, grasping for edges. And what chance did I stand against the ocean? How many times had the sea taken our captain and left her beating the shore with her hands?

It was an early lesson. The ocean disappears things. It is a hungry, grabbing thing. In its deep, there is nothing to reach for. Next to it, I was a girl gulping a woman's grief.

Jean Piaget believed object permanence to be learned within the first two years of life. That is, a thing disappeared continues to exist. But what if it never appears again? Or disappears long enough to learn to live without it? By two years old I had already learned two fathers. One addict. One sea captain. My birth father was Jon, a name like *him*, just a man. The Captain had two names: Robert for the merchant marine, and rounder Bob for his intimates. *Bob*, so close to *Dad*. Both taught me how to watch someone leave and not chase them.

When I asked my mother, *Why Melissa?* I already wanted a new name. Jackie, Britt, Tina. You can drill a hole with Jackie. You can slingshot a rock with Britt. Even Tina can hurt somebody. Melissa was bringing a ribbon to a sword-fight. Melissa was leading with my softest part.

A word shapes the mouth with want and wonder for its object. By six, I knew that Jessie down the street fit her name. Jessie was fast and blonde, a streak of girl, hook of *J*, dot of *i*, bared teeth of long *e*. It is no wonder that to hold *Jessie* in my mouth came to feel like holding Jessie in my mouth.

On her knees on the bedroom floor, Jessie pressed two naked dolls together, clicking their immovable parts. *What are they doing?* I asked. *You know*, she said. And I did, so I told her. I named the sex parts I knew. She repeated them back to me. Those strange sounds turned in the space between us. And they were ours.

I used to repeat words under my breath, on the way to school, in the bath, chanting their sounds until they detached from their meaning. The moment when those sounds fell free of their object—like the moment the swing hung horizontal to its frame, the body weightless, just before gravity clutched it back—giddying. It unlatched something in me, the proof that anything could be pulled apart, could scatter into dumb freedom, a bell ringing not for dinner or church or alarm, but for the simple pleasure of making it ring.

Just as Jessie and I chanted those words, unlocking the riddles of our bodies, I chanted my name. I pressed it against my teeth. To give it edges. To shake loose what it carried. To teach it meaning.

I learned the magic of repetition from Salinger's *Franny and Zooey*, which I found on a thrift store shelf, filmed with dust. I studied it as Franny Glass studied *The Way of a Pilgrim*, mesmerized by the idea of incessant prayer. Like me, Franny incanted a set of words—the Jesus Prayer— hoping to syncopate their intention with her heart's beat, the surge of her blood, turn even the mysterious work of her organs holy.

Lord Jesus Christ have mercy on me, goes the prayer.

Jesus was a cool guy, the Captain said. But religion was not. The nuns who swung wooden yardsticks against him and his brothers were not. My abuela told them to be good, to pray, to beg the help of no one but God. My abuelo had beaten them senseless. Help never came.

Praying to Jesus was not for anyone in our family. But I loved the word *mercy*. The idea of falling to one's knees moved something in me that I tended like a secret.

So I left out Jesus. *Have mercy on me*. Under my breath, on the way to school, in the ripped back seat of a white Subaru with a hand up my shirt, I waited to detach from the definition of my daily life, to feel the blooming quiet of something holier.

Even those ancient monks, writers of the *Philokalia*, believed that the repetition of words, and willingness, was all one needed. Faith could be summoned in the self, in saying, in the body. One didn't need to believe in God to walk toward God. I only had to believe in a word. So I started looking for it.

The Captain did not give me religion. He gave me other treasures. A bloom of desert roses the size of my arm, a freckled ostrich egg, true pirate stories. Jon, on the other hand, had given me native blood, which meant something only because it showed on my face. It was the one thing that reminded me of him, every time someone asked me, *What are you?*

I wished it had meant something to him, that he had given me a name I could decipher. Then everything might be different. He might be someone other than a drunk stranger living in a Florida trailer. And then who would I be?

My history seemed to end, or begin, with this name. Melissa. We packed those seven letters and a few boxes in the car. My mother and I drove away from him. We didn't take anything else. *Lucky*, I was told, to have wrecked so young, to have washed ashore with no memory.

True, I did not remember my first father. But forgetting, like leaving, does not erase someone. The Captain became the only dad I knew. And every time he left port, we wrecked again.

A new father brought me a new name. One from Puerto Rico.

The origin of Febos is not simple. There aren't many of us. My abuela told me that Febos was changed from *Febo*, because my great-grandfather thought it too close to *feo*, which means *ugly* in Spanish. A cute story. And a lie. Or myth, maybe. The uglier our own stories, the more some of us need pretty ones.

The Captain's grandfather, Amador, was a *jíbaro*— mountain-dwelling peasants, laborers of mixed indigenous Taino and Spanish blood who had worked alongside slaves on the cane, tobacco, and coffee plantations.

Amador, from the Latin *amare*, meaning *to love*. Ironic, as he was a *monstruo*. Or alcohol, and that breaking work, made him one. My guess: he was a lover. Sometimes the only cure for a soft heart is hard hands, or the elixirs that change them.

In the mountain village of Cayey, Taino for "a place of waters," the Captain's father, my grandfather, Modesto, at the age of seven, woke from sleep to find his father attempting to hang him by a noose from the ceiling. He never slept in Amador's house again, but under the cars of neighbors, returning days to care for his mother and younger siblings.

Modesto, from the Latin *modestus*, means "moderate, sober," though he also drank himself mad. The terrible legacy of his father was nothing a name could remedy. Those hard hands carved my own father, whose first mercy was the sea.

The Captain, on his voyages, made a habit of searching the phone books for *Febos*. The only reference he ever encountered was in Cervantes' *Don Quixote*, in which the Febos gang are a band of marauders who roam the Pyrenees.

He was looking for something, too.

At ten, in my bedroom, under alpaca blankets brought home by the Captain, I read the dictionary. I broke it open, the book an anchor sunk into my hips, each half covering a thigh. All afternoon I mouthed its wonders, this marvel I could open and close, soothed by the murmur of its onionskin pages.

Books were fickle ships, their mercy finite. The longer the better—*Roots*, *Clan of the Cave Bear*, *Les Misérables*, *Gone with the Wind*. I never wanted to go home. The twilight of stories fell like those of late autumn: all sweet and scary in their slipping, purpled shadows and smell of winter. Still I hurtled through them, my dread thickening as the remaining pages shrunk.

But the dictionary. All books held words, but the dictionary *was* words. It was a solar system of names, like the stars the Captain pointed out over our house: Polaris, Mizar, Arcturus, Vega, Mnemonic, Chasm, Nautilus. It pulsed from that low shelf in our living room, more magnetic than the crap black-and-white television on the old Singer sewing machine, than the fetal pig suspended in the jar in my science classroom. I looked into words as I looked up to those celestial bodies, calling out their names.

Mnemosyne. First generation Goddess, namer of all things. Titaness from whose own name we derived *mnemonic*, a word I loved for its swell—a wave of sound, the break of it. A word that moved but knew its own end.

Mnemosyne. When they met her, the dead faced a choice: drink from the river Lethe and forget the terror of this human life, or drink from the river Mnemosyne and remember. Those who drank to forget were reborn. Those who chose to remember continued, carting their dark histories across the western ocean to paradise.

Memory: my first drink. I stole a dusty bottle from my kitchen cabinet, labeled in a language I could not read. I poured that potion into me and felt the heat and churn of its work. I forgot myself. I forgot my mother leaving, this time, to live somewhere else. I forgot the Captain's grief, how it sank every object in our home: the desert rose, the ostrich egg, me. I forgot my own missing.

I drank to forget and I stopped caring where words came from. I stopped wondering what made them, what made me.

Something drew taut in me at twelve, and by fourteen it snapped. I said yes and no at all the wrong times. Yes of my thumb jut over Route 151, summoning the open door of an unknown car. Yes with a lighter flame held to anything that would burn. Yes to my friends' older brothers' hands and brother's friends' hands. Yes, yes, yes. *Is anything wrong?* No.

The summer before ninth grade, I kissed my best friend. By soccer season, I had no best friend. I cut off my hair. When a senior grabbed my breast in the hall between classes, I said nothing. I quit high school after one year. What could they teach me that I didn't already know? The Captain did not approve, but what else was new? He was a rule follower. Half the time he was gone. Soon, I would be, too.

I changed my name from Melissa with an *l*, to Melysa with a *y* and a single *s*. The double *s* had been a liability. That soft middle. All those curves. The small *i*—I'd found a way to cut it out of me. *Melissa* was unmoored, like the dinghies in the harbor that local boys hijacked and abandoned in the marsh grass, or left knocking against a far dock, oarless. An x, or a k, or a t would have been ideal, but I settled for y. Not barbed wire, but rope. *Melysa*, with that y, would stay tethered.

In the United States, approximately 17,000 people change their names each year. In nearly all states, "A person cannot choose a name that is intended to mislead." But what if one's given name is misleading? Melissa made promises I didn't want to keep.

Melysa with a y lasted a year. Occasionally I still find it printed inside the cover of a book. The first feeling is shame. Because I wanted to change myself? Or because I thought it would be that easy?

Shortening my name did not lessen me for long. I moved into the basement and Melissa swelled again to fill it. I read Plath and Lorde and lay on the floor and wished for Duras's lover. No, to *be* that lover. To say everything in so few words. I wished to be silent but blistered with sound. I breathed it into my dark basement, into girls' mouths, into my hands. I prayed for *such small hands* but I was a Hekatonkheir, hundred-handed and hungry. *You touch too hard*, said the first girl I loved. I rode my bike from ocean to ocean but her words followed me.

So I left home. And though I loved that dirty water, Boston was not box enough. Even New York could not quiet me.

Then heroin did. Drugs emptied me, refilled that space with vapors. Even the fiery melt of crack was an emptying: inhale it, and exhale the unseen self in a smoky swarm. The crackling splatter of me in that hot glass skillet—the abracadabra of evaporation.

How can I explain this? To hear my name and feel nothing. Freedom. Melissa became a mannequin of moveable parts. I could make her do anything. Dye my hair. Change my clothes. Answer an advertisement in the newspaper: *Young woman wanted for role-play and domination. Good money. No sex.* It was a challenge, and I had something to prove. Names meant nothing in that place. Melissa stepped into the elevator and Justine stepped out. It wasn't me. Those men could call me anything and I never flinched. It felt like choice.

At the end, when I had descended so far beyond the bare fact of myself that it was no longer escaped, but lost, I'd whisper into my cupped hand, *Melissa*. A caught bee, its familiar hum held to my ear. *Melissa*. I wanted to go home. I wanted a new word for *help*. I wanted a name for what remained underneath what I had become. It was the first time I admitted that Melissa might be such a name.

My mother kept bees when I was a girl. They lived in a white wooden hive behind her garden that resembled a chest of drawers. A small buzzing bureau. From the kitchen window, I could just make out the black specs of them, moving in and out, sometimes crawling on the face of it.

When she harvested, I stood in the yard and watched her careful movements. She wore head-to-toe white and a veiled hat—Victorian, astronautical—a bride of bees with a smoking can in her glove instead of flowers. Her hand on the bellows, smoke streamed from the spout, a potion to slow the bees as she plundered their hive.

She lifted out the frames so carefully, the ready combs heavy with honey and capped with wax. The bees' song swelled across the yard as they rested on her white arms and clung to the netting over her face.

With a knife's stroke she uncapped the comb and revealed each oozing hexagonal hole.

Sometimes, she handed me a broken comb and I held that warm hunk, its sweetness dripping down my forearm as I fought not to crush it, ached to close my hand around its torn geometry and feel its honey cover my knuckles.

Melissa fed the infant Zeus honey. That mountain nymph's bees delivered it straight into his mouth. This is the most common story, though there are many. I have looked for myself in all of them.

The bee nymph was known for introducing sweetness to men in the form of honey and thus taming them of eating one another. A civilizing influence. My mother didn't feed me sugar until I was nearly four years old. Honey was the only sweet my mouth knew and her undressed cakes more manna than any frosted future ones.

She tried. Honey might have tamed a different daughter. Sugar's grit might have better smoothed my wild. I suspect I would have eaten myself alive either way.

In other versions, Melissa hides the sticky-lipped baby to prevent him being eaten by his father, Cronus.

Find me a history without a monstrous father. Find me my father. There, in the shallow of our pond, dragging a metal rake, water darkening his cuffed pants. *He's at it again*, said my mother, shaking her head. He raked that muck all day, tried to beat it back and clear a path. But our pond was algae and animal—its murky depths could not be cleared. *It is a waste of time*, my mother said, *when there is so much to be done*. Overnight, the path disappeared. Again, he raked. My mother left him. Still, he kept raking. He did not crush gold cans of *Presidente*, like his father had. He did not collapse the drywall with our bodies. But I saw him weep in the yard. One hand on the fence, he folded over.

You are so lucky, he would say to me. I lay in bed and tried to make a prayer of it. *I am so lucky. I am so lucky.* Through the wall, I heard him scream in his sleep.

In this story, I was not the hider, but the hidden. My Captain is no monster. He tried to save me from those other devourers, but it was impossible. Even when we write our own stories there's no place to hide.

The sound of my name still shocks me. *Melissa*, and I startle, as if the sayer has called out to and seen some hidden part of me. It strikes me as both stranger and skeleton key; part cuss, part promise, part secret. *Melissa*, and I open sesame.

When lovers call my name—in the bathtub, in bed, over the telephone, or into my ear—it closes my eyes, buckles me, thralls my insides with the sweet terror of being recognized. Sometimes we cannot bear the thing we crave.

This is not a story about learning to love myself. My name is not a symbol. It is coded with all of this: the unseen, the near-known, the rather-not-known.

It hurts to hear everything my name holds, but I choose to drink from that river now, to carry that tangled history. I no longer want to change my name. I never did, really. I only wanted to know where I ended and everything else began, and I still do, in these oceanic days.

Like Franny Glass, I have begged of myself a prayer, begged of my name an answer. Made them the same powerful thing. Aren't they both gestures of surrender? Melissa may not be another word for mercy, but every name is a name for God.

LABYRINTHS

I waited outside of a methadone clinic in Bed-Stuy on a hot June morning in 2002. New York was already steeped in the smell of cooking garbage. I bought three doses off a jaundiced junkie, the whites of his eyes gone yolk. The scalped methadone came in liquid form and its chemical silt collected on the bottom of the plastic container. I poured it into a bottle of grape Gatorade and got on the gypsy bus in Chinatown for a fifteen-dollar ride to Boston.

I was headed back to my mother's and hoping to get clean before starting my final semester of college. I had been shooting up for two years. But she didn't know that.

That summer, my brother and I split our time between the big old house north of Cambridge that my mother shared with her fiancé and the Cape Cod home of our childhood, which sat on the edge of a pond nestled in the woods. My second day in Boston, I wedged my mickeyed Gatorade bottle in the back of my mother's freezer and thought, *Just one more*. Every weekend, I drove to see a boy on the North Shore. We got high, listened to vinyl albums of Miles Davis and Patti Smith in front of the air conditioner, and I took home enough glassine baggies to last until my next visit.

When we were both home, my brother and I made microwave quesadillas and watched TV. It was a reenactment of our late-childhood pastime. We were not allowed to watch television as kids except in short approved doses. Instead, we repeatedly viewed a small collection of VHS tapes, choice among which was *Labyrinth*, starring a teenaged Jennifer Connelly, David Bowie as Jareth the Goblin King, and a supporting cast of Jim Henson puppets. For every time we watched *E.T.* or *The Sound of Music*, we watched *Labyrinth* ten times.

Back then, we sat for hours, silently unwinding and rewinding that tape. We curled on opposite ends of the love seat in our den and never spoke about our troubles. Both then and now, I found comfort in proximity if not confidence. In both cases it was as close as I got to anyone.

Boston oozed under a layer of humidity that curled our hair and glistened our faces. One afternoon we watched a marathon of *Freaks and Geeks*, Judd Apatow's smart series about teenagers in the 1980s that was canceled after one season. It featured a brother and sister whose relationship bore a striking resemblance to ours.

A meaty black fly kept landing on my neck and the touch of its tiny legs sent chills down my back. I periodically jammed my knuckles into my thigh to soothe an ache in my quadriceps. I could do nothing about the eye-twitch, or the terrifying fact that I was broke and growing more dopesick with each passing minute.

My brother was restless, too. At some point, he became too restless to watch TV. He wanted to talk. His brows drew together in concentration. My brother's eyes are green like mine but bigger and darker and framed by thick lashes. As a little boy, he had had a huge head and those same enormous eyes. We all called him Boo, a name that I'd given him on the day of his birth. That afternoon, his eyes glowered, pleaded. He wanted to explain something to me, or needed me to explain it to him. His six-foot-two body moved self-consciously, hands damp against his furred knees, ruined skate sneakers planted on the floor. He described a recent afternoon in the backyard when he had tried to give himself a haircut. The handheld mirror had broken and he had cut himself on a shard. Something about the blood. I couldn't understand what he was trying to tell me and we both grew frustrated.

His handsome face clouded. I wondered when the dark circles under his eyes had appeared. There was a thunder in him. The pressure of a storm gathering. I was sealed in my own trouble. I couldn't help him.

Labyrinth also features a sister and her younger brother. The film begins with Sarah, a spoiled, fanciful fifteen-year-old girl who resents her half brother, the infant Toby. Consigned to a night of babysitting, she spitefully invents a story, the sobbing baby in her arms. "There once was a poor girl," she begins, and tells Toby about a Goblin King who is in love with the girl, and who longs to take the baby away if only she utters the right words. And Sarah does. Toby disappears and is replaced by a snowy owl who transforms into the Goblin King.

Made in 1986, the aesthetic of *Labyrinth* reflects the era, but my MTV-sheltered eyes had seen nothing like it. Feathered and leathered, the ethereal Jareth juggled crystal balls and spoke in riddles. He was part woman, thin and tortured with skintight pants and so much desire locked inside him. He hated her. He needed her. I saw it in the wounded cruelty of his face as he showed Sarah the labyrinth he'd make her solve in order to retrieve her brother. My heart raced as I beheld that sprawling puzzle, a glowing desert of pathways, a spired castle at its center.

"It doesn't look that far," Sarah lied.

"It's farther than you think," he said.

Unlike Sarah, I never resented my brother. He had always felt like mine. We had different birth fathers but had been raised by the same man. I never thought of the Captain as my *adoptive* father. And I never thought of my brother as my half brother.

Like me, he was born at home—all ten pounds of him, in June of 1984, surrounded by midwives and sunshine. My mother moaned as that big head split her open, squeezing the Captain's hands bloodless. When I tell people that I was present at my brother's birth, I am sometimes met with looks of horror. As an adult, I can see how such an experience might traumatize some almost-four-year-olds. But on the cassette tapes recorded that day, over my mother's grunts and the encouraging murmurs of her coaches, my own small voice rings out elatedly. In the photos I kneel beside her naked body, a toy stethoscope dangling from my ears, one pudgy hand pressing the diaphragm to her chest. I probably thought I delivered him.

In our house, we knew the correct names for body parts. But we never said *shut up*, never called someone *stupid*. My brother and I rarely fought. We invented games and read stories and played dress-up with the trunk of exotic costumes that the Captain had collected in his travels. Sometimes, at the dinner table, as we laughed and laughed over some joke known only to us, I caught a glimpse of envy on my mother's face.

Behind his bedroom door, my brother built Lego cities, assembled costumes made entirely of duct tape and cardboard toilet paper rolls. He was Hiawatha, with an athletic-sock quiver and wooden stirring-spoon arrows. He was a Ninja Turtle, with cardboard shell and red-rag bandanna. He was the gentlest creature I knew, trying night after night to make himself into a warrior with the detritus of our home.

Back then, I hid toys and household objects, delighted by my private knowledge of their whereabouts. Philosopher and ethicist Sissela Bok claims that, "To be able to hold back some information about oneself, or to channel it and thus influence how one is seen by others gives power," and in a theory echoed by Winnicott, Piaget, and Carl Jung, sees a child's early revelation of silence as a necessary differentiation of the self.

Jung describes his own formative experience of devising a diorama of a "little manikin" he had carved, with matching bed and coat, all of which he kept hidden from others. "No one could discover my secret and destroy it," he explains. "I felt safe, and the tormenting sense of being at odds with myself was gone." I had no words for this, but reading his confession as an adult, I knew exactly that relief.

Before Sarah summons the Goblin King and enters the labyrinth, she spends her days reciting poetry, imagining herself a tragic heroine. Like Sarah, I was dramatic, and spent hours lost in fantasy. She was infatuated with her own beauty, and I so much wanted to be beautiful. But when I watch the film for the first time in twenty years, what strikes me most, alongside her self-absorption, is her anger.

"It's not fair!" she shouts again and again. She kicks the walls of the labyrinth in fits of entitled rage. My brother and I watched, dumbfounded, relieved by distraction. We were not angry. We missed the Captain. We didn't know how to cure our mother's sadness or our own. We only knew how to pour it into the hours of familiar stories. And *Labyrinth* was the most compelling.

My brother, especially, showed the effects of the Captain's months at sea. He followed me everywhere. I believed, as my parents did, that I was less troubled and so his protector. But no one could protect my brother from himself. He suffered from terrible nightmares. They came every night for the first two weeks after the Captain's departures. My brother woke wailing from dreams of Chucky, the murderous doll from the 1988 horror movie *Child's Play*. A wooden nutcracker figurine that we brought out during the holidays tormented him. In sleep, my brother's fear of abandonment took the shapes of scarecrows and toys. His imagination animated them with the same vividness of his art projects and Lego creations. My brother, the creator. The boy alchemist. His tear-stained face and wet lashes pressed against my mother's chest, inconsolable. I stroked his soft hair. When our babysitters tried to put him to bed, he screamed and ran out into the street.

A boy needs his father, I once heard my mother say into the telephone. I turned those words in my mind. I barricaded myself in books and secrets. I waited to become a teenager, waited to become beautiful, waited for my own Goblin King.

I was sad, too. Just a few years away from chaos, from the end of my body as I knew it, I was already itchy, brooding, watching myself cry in the mirror without knowing why.

One afternoon, I shut my bedroom door in his face. He pummeled it and I flung the door open. There he stood red-faced, cheeks streaked with tears, heaving with the Hulk-ish fury of the powerless.

I hate you, I said. I shut the door.

Hours later I emerged. The day had just tipped from blue into black and a few reflected lights flickered on the surface of the pond. My brother sat in an old armchair and his face shone with tears.

Mom said that big sisters aren't allowed to hate their little brothers, he said, through anguished hiccups.

We all carry a small catalog of unsealable wounds. Maybe these breaches of conscience that retain their power to sear are necessary reminders of our own boundaries. We touch them to remember. To prevent future transgression. But no sting compares to this one. It carved something out of me. A space that filled with the shocking light of how much I could hurt the person I least wanted to. It was the first love that made sense of the word *tender*, which refers not only to a gentle feeling, but to the ache and vulnerability of loving someone. Which is not the same thing as protecting them.

In the summer of 2002, my brother was angry. He had spent his senior year of high school brooding, stoned, painting self-portraits that now hang on the wall of our mother's house, beautiful and chilling reminders of that summer. He won an all-city award for high school artists, and was accepted by a prestigious art college in Baltimore.

My mother was planning her wedding. Her fiancé was a scholar, a man brilliant and funny and sometimes mean. She was looking for a way out of marrying him, but didn't know it yet. My brother was readying to leave for college in August and had just quit smoking pot. Then, he stopped sleeping.

He didn't like my mother's fiancé. He didn't like the way he spoke to her or to us. *I'm sick of being patronized,* he complained. The Captain was planning a move to the furthest corner of the country from us under the misguided impression that we might follow. He had retired from the sea and still we rarely saw him. I was too sunk in my own addiction to care, but my brother had never stopped wanting more from him. He stomped up and down the stairs. He slammed doors and drawers. The world was fucked up and so was our family and he was done pretending otherwise.

Anger made his body so animal. It seemed the force of it might split him open. I was afraid to touch him, my little brother, afraid of how badly he might need that. I wished he could pull it together. My addiction was ugly, but no one else had to see. My brother was spilling everywhere and it scared me as only a glimpse of our secret selves can scare.

One afternoon, my mother and I made plans to brunch the next morning. The only safe topic by then was our shared worry over my brother. That night I borrowed her car and went on an all-night drug binge. On the early morning drive home, I came to as my car tires bumped over the sidewalk, my front fender grinding against the fence of the high school athletic field. I crept into my basement room and slept for twelve hours. The next afternoon I staggered into the kitchen and found my mother at the table with her hands wrapped around a cup of tea. Her face was so lonely in the moment before she looked up and saw me. Her familiar shape in the chair a dead weight in my chest.

What's going on with you? she asked me.

I think I'm coming down with something, I said.

That month, she developed a sudden and debilitating case of psoriatic arthritis. Her knees swelled and throbbed until she could barely climb the stairs of our home.

I want to be able to dance at my own wedding, she said, and postponed it indefinitely.

One afternoon, I drove my brother to his friend's house. I pushed a mixtape into the cassette player and the opening bass notes of a favorite PJ Harvey song twanged. My brother turned up the volume. He nodded his head and when I looked at him, he smiled at me for the first time in a long time.

This is amazing, he said.

He kept smiling. That note of wonderment burrowed into his voice and took seed.

That's amazing, he said, listening to the peepers chirrup in the pond as late summer drew over us.

That's amazing, about a broken chair along the highway between Cape Cod and Boston that he made me pull over to inspect.

He's being so nice, my mother whispered.

I nodded. I wanted to feel as relieved as she looked.

The word *amaze* gives us *maze*, from Middle English, denoting delirium or delusion. To be *mazed* is to be confused, stupefied, lost. The noun, of course, is a puzzle—a complex network of passages through which one has to find a way.

And so my brother seemed—mazed, amazed, trapped in a puzzle. He wandered the rooms of our house. He unpacked art supplies to begin projects and left them scattered across the floor. He stood on the shore of our pond and marveled. He wrote page after page in an old spiral-bound notebook. He asked us so many questions, but his gaze shifted as we answered, ever distracted by the next turn and what lay around its corner.

In the beginning, the labyrinth looks to Sarah like an infinite corridor. She runs and runs and then, frustrated, kicks the glistening bricks, chest heaving. But then she realizes there are openings all around her—Greek walls, hedges, misty groves, and toxic bogs. At first, this discovery exhilarates her; she is trapped not in a monolithic dungeon or an endless hallway to nowhere, but in a fantastical world full of choices. Ebullient, she bounds through a doorway and falls into a pit. She has mistaken her changed perception of the labyrinth for the labyrinth's changing. However altered its appearance, she is still trapped; the labyrinth's many magical turns are an illusion created by the Goblin King.

Though they are used interchangeably, mazes and labyrinths are not synonymous. A maze is characterized by many possible paths, dead ends, and digressions. A labyrinth is unicursal and has only one path to its center. By these definitions, all Sarah has to do to "solve" the labyrinth is keep going. Her real challenge is to ignore the Goblin King's illusory distractions. Throughout the film Jareth tries to convince her that the labyrinth is too difficult to solve. He drugs her. He sends creatures to mislead her. He promises her that happiness is in succumbing to his fantasy and abandoning her quest to solve the labyrinth.

"I ask for so little," he pleads. "Just let me rule you, and you can have everything that you want."

I recognized the seeming romance of my brother's mania. Drugs had also felt like a doorway to a fantastical world of choices. For thirty dollars I could go anywhere without fear. Heroin, especially, leveled the relative danger and value of all things.

A routine day in my college years included a morning class for which I was always well prepared. I attended study groups and rehearsals of our college chorus. I interned at the

Rockefeller Center offices of a national magazine. I drank tiny cups of wheatgrass and ran on treadmills at the local YMCA. Then I met my dealer on the way home and bought three bags of dope and three bags of crack, because while I preferred cocaine it was harder to find in Bed-Stuy. I locked myself in my bedroom. I dissolved the crack with lemon juice and shot speedballs by candlelight so that my roommates wouldn't know that I was home. I sometimes cradled the telephone on my shoulder so that if I overdosed I might have time to dial 911.

I have called my former logic "junkie arithmetic." It was a kind of mental magic that allowed the performance of functionality to excuse my life-threatening secrets.

While he acknowledges the crucial role of secrecy in his childhood, Jung also states that the keeping of secrets can act like a psychic poison and alienate their possessor from the community. And Bok agrees that the freedom and power acquired in secrecy can backfire. When an idea is isolated from the feedback and perception of others, she explains that "secrecy can debilitate judgment and choice, spread, and become obsessive." The secret space becomes a prison in which moral judgment and logic are starved and development arrests.

As the days passed, my brother's pupils spread over the green of his eyes like night settling on our pond. Ideas roiled in him and spilled onto broad sheets of paper. He scrawled them furiously in the notebook that he now carried everywhere. He found and filled with his papers an old briefcase. This he guarded fastidiously. He grew thin. He began to look like someone battling something.

My brother is a June baby. A Gemini. A majority of the people I have loved were born under the sign of the twins, Castor and Pollux, and have characters marked by their alleged binary qualities. The twins are often said to have been born from an egg with their half sisters: Helen of Troy and Clytemnestra. And like those mythological sisters, the brother I wanted to save ended up saving me.

One night he stood in our kitchen. Around him lay scattered pens and paper, shards of torn cardboard, a scattering of chalk, the briefcase. Through an open window the smell of woods, a choir of crickets. Lit from behind, he towered, a shimmering hologram of that boy I'd seen born eighteen years earlier. He stared through me and the dark windows into something I couldn't see.

In ancient Greece, a double incidence of St. Elmo's fire was coined after the celestial twins. The weather phenomenon occurs most often on ship masts during storms and sailors have long known it for a bad omen. Darwin saw one aboard the *Beagle*, Starbuck in Melville's *Moby Dick*, and Prospero in *The Tempest*. If an electrical field grows strong enough a sphere of glowing plasma throws a coronal light that appears like blue flames on ship masts, turrets, even the horns of animals. In 1899, Nikola Tesla described creating one in his lab as he tested a Tesla coil. "Butterflies became electrified and 'Helplessly swirled in circles—their wings spouting halos of St. Elmo's fire.'"

I saw that fire blaze on the mast of my brother. But he saw that blaze in everything. There in our kitchen he was both butterfly and mad inventor, captive to his creation.

My mother watched us so closely. And she was a psycho-therapist. But love that great always includes blind spots. Maybe it requires them. *I knew something was wrong*, she tells me now. There is a hesitation in this statement. She did not want to see it. Eventually, it became impossible to ignore his worsening. She made an appointment for him with a psychiatrist who came recommended.

One day she was driving through Boston with him. My brother's restless knees jumped. His eyes flitted around the car and bore into the car in front of them. When my mother stopped at a red light, my brother opened the passenger door and got out of the car. He began walking away from her with the briefcase in his hand. She called out to him and he stopped. *Where are you going?* she asked. He wouldn't say.

Please get back in the car, she said. He refused. *Please,* she said. *I need you to get back in the car.* After a moment, he obeyed.

My mother then held her private practice in an office adjacent to our home on the Cape. During one of my mother's sessions, my brother's naked upper body bobbed by the window directly behind her patient's back.

It's almost funny, now, she admits. *I mean, what the hell was he doing?* She pauses. *But it wasn't funny at the time.*

He soon explained, his body scribbled red from the brambles in the woods near our home. He'd retreated into the woods when a suspicious truck pulled up at the house, and then swum across our pond and lost his shorts.

Who is chasing you? our mother asked.

My brother's theory was that all people have an electrical component to their thoughts and emotions and if one is sensitive enough, or pays attention in the right way, one can pick up on this electricity and read others' minds. In his words, he was *trying to put the seemingly transcendent energy and intellectual excitement of my experience to a practical use in looking at scientific blind spots*. If he had discovered this capacity to mind-read, he reasoned, then certainly the government knew. He was a danger to the state, who would want to stop him from sharing this revelation with the world.

My brother has, years later, described to me his awareness back then that many of his suspicions might be paranoia. He trusted that some of his thoughts were true, but describes his flight from the mysterious truck as a hedging of bets in the case that he wasn't paranoid. He knew what direction my mother's clients faced and made the choice to streak by her window, knowing that only she would see him. *I did the best I could not to freak anyone out*, he has told me.

His self-awareness, that juggling of possible realities impresses me both with its conscientiousness and its burden. It is difficult for me to imagine that state of being—not because it is inconceivable to me, but because it is so painful. And despite his conscientiousness, we were still freaked out. Whatever had opened him so wide, now it seemed to be crushing him.

The figures of his boyhood nightmares returned. Chucky and the Nutcracker. Like the goblins in *Labyrinth*, these figures were the henchmen of my brother's fear, both symptoms and agents of his own crumbling illusion. Except this time, instead of enacting his terror at our captain's absence, they signified a different abandonment. They haunted the space where his own self had been.

I didn't think he was sure that no one chased him or that our phones weren't bugged. But to me he seemed skeptical enough to try believing us. Though it was painful to behold, I was grateful for his uncertainty. His fear, even. I thought it softened his resistance to the doctor's prescriptions. That, and our mother's fiancé issued an ultimatum that my brother take the meds or move out of their house.

My brother has since told me that it was not his own fear that motivated him to take the medications, but ours. The choice to take the meds or leave my mother's house was not one he made easily, and one that he made primarily to appease us.

He slept for such a long time.

They diagnosed him with bipolar disorder. He was eighteen and right on schedule for when the first true manic episode strikes most sufferers. The literature that I read also stated that most future bipolar patients experience episodes of depression throughout childhood. It is easy in retrospect to say that he was a depressed child. That I was. But that word and the others that followed were not a part of our vocabulary back then. My brother and I were only ourselves:

sad and conflicted, vivacious and inspired. The nickname I had given him when he was born, Boo, was a better word. That single syllable still carries all of it. That beautiful boy I saw born and the man he became. All the brilliant pain and miracle of him. How could I have defined him by any word that did not include my love for him?

This is the slippery nature of diagnoses and the reason my brother became so rightfully suspicious of them. Pathology comforts in its reductiveness, but is no true authority, just a bunch of words invented by men. A list of compiled symptoms. Categorization and definition facilitate analysis, but conflation is dangerous and difficult to avoid. My brother can be described as bipolar the same way he can be described as *artist, Gemini, introvert, brother*. To limit him to any one of these contextual references erases him.

His depression had also not occurred to me because I had been busy thinking about myself. My brother's diagnosis came with one for me as well: fraud. I had always considered myself his protector, but I had failed to see so much. In my secrecy and self-absorption, I had protected only myself.

Addiction runs in our family. The Captain's father was a mean drunk. And my birth father, Jon, is an addict. Madness is also our legacy. My mother's father was also bipolar, or manic depressive, as they used to call it. Though they didn't call it anything but *gone* in his case. He abandoned his family when my mother was four. He died a recluse, holed up in a book-lined room in Jacksonville, Florida.

My end would have been similar. I always imagined that if it got bad enough my family would stage an intervention. I wouldn't be able to hide it. But I would have died before reaching that moment of visibility. The moment that I glimpsed this fact was sheer grace. Nothing else could have pierced my illusion.

I was alone in my bedroom in Brooklyn with a dwindling pile of heroin and a few crumbs of crack that I was dissolving with lemon juice to shoot speedballs. I tasted citrus with each shot, the surging high like a hand on the back of my neck in whose grip I went limp. It was a night like many others. But in the midst of this one the veil suddenly lifted, and I was struck by the terrifying truth: I was not waiting to be saved. I was waiting to die.

How had I ever thought I was less vulnerable than my brother? What an old and shallow trick—to judge your insides by someone else's outsides. For a long time, I cherished my ability to conceal my trouble. Later on, my brother's inability to hide his own seemed a much more valuable gift.

After the doctors, the diagnosis, the arguments spiked with terror—*Stop talking about me!* he'd yell from the next room, *You've been doing that my whole life!*—I drove my brother and his new prescriptions to the Cape. I was mildly dopesick again. My slick hands slid around the wheel and my knee jittered on the clutch. My brother stared at the muddy bumper of the car in front of us. He spoke slowly.

Maybe some things aren't real, but the rest is. He picked at his ragged fingernails, each crowned with a stripe of dirt. *Their diagnoses are bullshit. They pretend God wrote the* DSM *or something.*

I agreed with him, but it didn't matter. I just wanted him to take those pills and come back to himself.

The world is fucked up, he went on. *But they want me to take pills so I'll keep accepting it.*

The world *was* fucked up. But I wanted to take pills to keep accepting it. Not only did my brother remain earnest in his madness, but his madness actually seemed an expression of it.

You can't hold all that in your mind at once, Boo, I said. Rain speckled the windshield and I flicked on the wipers. *I think our psyches develop ways of modulating how much we can take in. They know that we can only handle a certain amount of truth at once.* I didn't elaborate on the ways this function had gone haywire in my own circuitry. I glanced at him. His hand gripped the passenger armrest as he stared straight ahead. *I feel like you've lost that somehow*, I said. *You're getting too much.*

After a pause, he asked, *You see that car in front of us?*

Yeah.

It's probably not following us, right?

Probably not.

I steered the car toward the beach instead of home, our bodies leaning together as the road curved. I pulled into the beach parking lot and the silence swelled around us when I killed the engine. My brother scratched his head and sighed. I could feel the tension radiate from his body. My hands in my lap and his length folded tautly in the passenger seat, we stared at the choppy water.

I've always loved the Atlantic, I said. *It's so broody. I don't think I could ever live in California. The Pacific is too glamorous.*

Right, he said. *What with the never-ending party of the Pacific Trash Vortex.*

I laughed and he smiled a little.

Waves broke against a jetty, its rocky finger pointed toward the horizon. The rain slowed.

I know you want to see clearly, I said. *To not depend on chemicals for the rest of your life.*

He nodded. *I think there has to be another way*, he said.

But Boo, I said, turning to him now, *if you don't, you will be dependent on Mom and Dad, instead. On doctors you don't trust. On hospitals.* Tears pressed behind my eyes and I made myself turn to look at him.

Our eyes met and I saw that his were also wet. His pupils were still wide as wells that ran to the bottom of him. The ring of green around them mirrored the sea all around us—inconsolable and dazzling. He nodded, whether in agreement or resignation, I didn't know.

My biggest fear was that my brother would stay mad. Bipolar people are notorious for going off their meds—the thrill of mania is too alluring. The rates of suicide are estimated as high as one in every five diagnosed with bipolar. I believed what I said to him. I also know that I would have said anything to get him to take those drugs.

The ways in which I understood his madness also scared me. The fearsome qualities of my own mind had always felt like another secret I kept. I understood the logic of his argument: that the conventions of modern human civilization were as crazy as any madman's delusion, they just had a consensus. But I also knew the power of my own imagination, the way my mind could nurture an image, escalate it into a weapon to use against myself. And on some level, even then, I understood that my own affliction was as twisted. If he stayed lost in his labyrinth then what hope was there for me? I could not even speak of my trouble.

But my hubris was already weakened. It was not up to me to convince my brother of anything. It was not I, nor anyone, who would keep him from a life of madness, or show him the way back. As the poet Denise Levertov said, "One can anyway only be shown something one knows already, needs already. *Showing* anyone anything really amounts to removing the last thin film that prevents their seeing what they are looking at." My protection and power over him had always been a story I told myself for my own comfort.

The labyrinth, after all, is Sarah's creation. She calls upon the Goblin King. And this is the biggest difference between my brother's afflictions and mine: whatever the biological and historical factors, I still chose mine. And I chose to keep it a secret from the people who would have helped me. It is a pattern that has followed me all my life—from drugs, to sex work, to mad love. I have always chosen my poisons. The things that will hurt and grow me the most.

In *Labyrinth*, Sarah believes she is on a mission to save her brother. But Toby is a MacGuffin. The real quest is for our heroine's own transformation. By solving the labyrinth, Sarah smashes her self-absorption, her denial, her estrangement from the people who love her.

Like her, there was only one person I needed to save: myself.

After my brother finally slept, but before his mind settled, he asked me to come up to his room.

I need you to look under the bed, he said.

I nodded and got down on my knees. I looked hard at the crooked floorboards, a sideways crate of records, some clumps of dust and hair.

There's nothing there, I told him.

He nodded and sat on the edge of the bed. I sat next to him. I slid my big hand into his big hand and squeezed.

It would have been tempting, once, to make myself the hero of this scene—to admire my own power to rescue my brother. But the real power here is his, in knowing what he needed and in asking for my help.

There is a scene in *Labyrinth* where Sarah awakens in a sprawling junkyard, an infinite dump. Dazed, she turns to a goblin woman with heaps of trash piled on her, "I was searching for something."

The woman hands Sarah her own teddy bear. "That's what you were looking for, wasn't it, my dear?" she says. She leads

Sarah through a door into a perfect replica of her own bedroom. Sarah throws herself on her bed in relief. "It was all a dream," she says. "But it was so real." She tries to walk out the door into her own house and the woman stops her.

"Better to stay in here, dear," she says, and begins handing Sarah her familiar treasured things. "Your little bunny rabbit! You like your little bunny rabbit?" She reminds Sarah of the fantasies she once valued over the people in her life. Sarah takes the dolls, but repeats, "There was something I was looking for." With a surge of conviction she pushes her way out of the false bedroom into the junkyard, once again determined to find Toby.

Sarah was ungrateful. She was fanciful. She wanted escape. She wanted to be worshiped. All Jareth's promises were tailored to her desires. But she could not accept them. Over and over, some inscrutable part of her could not give in, could not betray what was true in her by accepting a false paradise buried in a junkyard.

It is a perfect analogy of addiction. Of redemption from any illusion. Call it grace, call it survival, call it strength—whatever allowed me to seize that moment of clarity and insist that what I was searching for was not in any cloistered room. It is something that my brother and I were given by our parents and the ways that they loved us. It is a fundamental belief in the worth of one's own life. It is the knowledge of true love, and the belief that we are capable givers and receivers of it.

When Sarah finally reaches the castle at the center of the labyrinth, Jareth makes his final plea to her: "Just fear me, love me, do as I say, and I will be your slave." It is the song of every seductive captor, every addiction, every fearful lover, every shadowed history. Sarah finally knows that it is she who will be the slave, and his power only exists if she believes in it. The power has been hers all along. She understands this as my mother did when she left her fiancé. As I did when I finally gave up heroin.

"You have no power over me," Sarah says, and the labyrinth breaks into pieces.

My own liberation was not so fast. Neither was my brother's.

A year after my brother broke apart, I flew across the country and met him in Olympia, Washington. He'd deferred college for a year and spent it living there with a close friend. I had missed him that year and when it ended, I suggested that I fly out to meet him. Together we could drive all his belongings back east, where he would start school in the fall. In our mother's battered Ford Escort station wagon with an old boom box duct-taped to the dashboard, we drove across the country in five days. He had gone off his meds a couple of times that year and I had gone to some twelve-step meetings. We were both frayed. We were both climbing out of something.

We stopped first in San Francisco to visit my girlfriend—a woman I'd dated in college who had been at the bad end of my erratic behavior but had agreed to one more round. We left my brother at her parents' house and stayed out all night snorting coke. The morning's hangover was laden with guilt. While we'd been out partying, my brother had taken himself up to Twin Peaks alone and stared out at the foggy city. Before we left, I wrote a letter to a different ex-girlfriend and explained how well I was doing. *I'm going to AA meetings*, I said, which was technically true.

My brother was sullen on that day's drive. Our conversation circled and dead-ended. He spoke in fits and then stared sulkily at the smear of passing highway and trees. I was anxious and suggested that we stop and get a drink. He wasn't interested. I feared our whole trip would continue like this. I feared that in our breaking, we had broke something between us.

Late that night we wound through Big Sur. The headlights illuminated redwood trunks thick as houses. Those trees and the darkness felt more solid than anything in me. We might have been the only two people on earth. I felt desperate to reach through the clotted silence between us. I missed him so much, this person I'd known his whole life, who knew me in ways no one else ever could.

I want to tell you something, I said.

Yeah?

I have a drug problem, I said. My ears rung with fear.

You do? he said.

Yeah, I said. *I'm going to meetings, but I haven't totally stopped yet.* I slowed around a steep curve and the wind slapped a leaf against my window.

Wow, he said.

It's really fucking hard, I said. Tears instantly fell down my cheeks. It was such a relief to finally say it aloud.

We sat in silence for a few more winding turns. He looked at me.

I'm glad you told me, he said. His voice had softened. *You always acted so together. Like everything was easy for you.*

Really? I sputtered a nervous laugh.

Yeah. It made it really hard to relate to you.

Together, huh? I laughed for real then and so did he. I felt something seep out of him, and out of me. Giddy with the sudden ease, I took a deep breath. We looked at each other in the dark and started laughing all over again.

The rest of the trip we ate Krispy Kreme donuts and cracked each other up just like when we were kids. As we stared over the edge of the Grand Canyon, I sighed theatrically. *I thought it would be better*, I said. My brother doubled over. He took a picture of me shrugging with the canyon behind me. We camped that night and he made me laugh so hard that I peed in my sleeping bag. As we crossed the bottom of the Mojave Desert, I took a photograph of my brother standing beside the highway, endless dry earth stretching out behind him like an emptied sea.

Over the next several years, my brother worked his way off of the meds. He was right that there were other ways to ease himself. He has not suffered a manic episode for many years. He still struggles in ways that I attribute to the part of him that he silenced. And that he attributes to that silencing. Our memories of that time are so different.* Of course they are. In my mind, my brother narrowly avoided institutionaliza-tion. Though he once said to me, *maybe I would have ended up in a psych ward, but at least I would have gotten there following what I believed.* I wanted to answer him, but at what cost? Though I understood. Perhaps I am uniquely qualified to understand. I have always been driven to find my own limits, and have often found them in dark places. But I

° My brother's own account of these events and more information can be found here: www.sustainabeast.com/fundamental-illness

was more scared for him than I have ever been for myself. This is one of love's many hypocrisies. I want the people I love to do not as I would or have done, but whatever will keep them safe. That is, whatever will not break my heart. We were scared, yes, terrified. And fear narrows our vision. But the choice was still his to make.

I don't know that I would do anything different if I could, even if my brother wishes I had. I cannot ever know his truth from the inside. I can only know my own. It was not only a thing that happened to my brother. It was a thing that happened to me. To all of us. Our family was forever changed and maybe there will never be a way to reconcile our different stories. We may never trust each other as we once did, or could have. There is a sorrow in me deeper than the regret of any cruelty for the fact of this: none of us could have protected each other. We could not even have protected ourselves. And though it is not a solution or a salve, there is also freedom in this humility. One that I did not have before.

The year after our cross-country trip, I got clean for real. That moment of confidence with my brother was a kind of map—an indication of what I would have to do over and over, for the rest of my life. In the decade of sobriety that has followed, I have replaced my instinct for secrecy with an instinct for confession.

There are still times when he and I fall into our respective labyrinths. I no longer believe that anyone but ourselves can lead us out. The Minotaurs we need to rescue are never our half brothers. They are always those monstrous parts of ourselves. We can never even know for certain that we are free. The best we can offer each other, and ourselves, is a few honest words.

ALL OF ME

We are in her bed and she props herself up on one elbow. Her bangs are tangled. Her forehead is damp and her face is soft. We have just made love, and the sun is rising. It glows through the drawn curtains of her bedroom with desert light.

What about this one? she asks, lifting my arm and brushing the inside of my wrist with her fingertips.

My little brother's nickname.

And this? she touches the anatomical heart on my forearm, and smiles. *Heart on your sleeve?*

I like to remember that it's a muscle, I say.

Her hand slides over the crook of my elbow and grasps my bicep. *This is my favorite*, she says. It is a portrait of Billie Holiday. She is in mid-song. Her features are finely detailed in black. It is my favorite, too.

I inevitably guide new lovers through a tour of my tattoos. It's a sweet milestone and an easy way to introduce them to my story without having to volunteer unsolicited intimacies. Easier to hand someone a map than to show them where it leads.

We all want this in love—for our lovers to spot the marks of our losses, the scars that note how we have been changed, how we became the person they love. It's not easy to offer these details. Sometimes, it is impossible. My tattoos make the first move.

They are also an invitation to strangers, who reach for me through this social loophole on the subway, the sidewalk, in cafes and gyms. The pull of an illustrated body overrides even classroom hierarchies, and sometimes my students lean so close to inspect the images decorating my shoulders that I can feel their breath on me. Not only do my tattoos erase the invisible membrane between our bodies, but they also dissolve what manners prevent strangers from commenting on others' bodies.

I understand the impulse. I have willfully exposed something that draws their attention and thus invited it. The same flawed logic drives men in the street to whistle, hiss, honk, or comment on the bodies of passing women, though I offer them no such pass. Their impulse is also one to remind me of their power. I did not choose my female body. But I chose every image painted on it.

Billie Holiday's voice first spoke to me as a girl. Though a

gregarious child, I became an anguished adolescent—
sensitive, empathic, secretive, and sexual. The marriage of
pain and sweetness in her crooning hit notes I couldn't
approximate in language or any bodily expression. Books
were my obsession, but music more succinctly captured
emotion than any combination of words I found. The nights I
didn't spend reading by flashlight, I curled around the radio,
finger over the *record* button. I filled blank cassettes with
songs I'd replay over and over and over. But Billie's voice was
best. She sounded haunted and at twelve and thirteen, I felt
haunted, visited by surges of feeling invisible on my outsides.

I was already calling myself a writer. I furiously scrawled
poems in notebooks. I romanticized my angst and toted
Kerouac and Anaïs Nin around in my backpack. I guarded my
vulnerabilities but longed to externalize them. Writing was
the obvious choice. But music was the shortcut. Learning an
instrument appeared too laden in technique, so I asked my
mother for voice lessons.

My singing teacher's name was Shirley. Round and blonde,
with an upturned nose and equestrian penchant, she ran
scales with me every Wednesday after school in a stuffy room
above our town's only guitar shop. Though gifted with range,
volume, and feeling, my pitch needed work. I loathed practicing to the cassettes we recorded of exercises. Listening to
my own voice stagger up and down the scales filled me with

a tedious embarrassment. I wanted only the rush of breath from my heart to my mouth.

Shirley wanted me to sing from the books of *singers*, women who sprawled across their book covers in long skirts, kitten heels, and artfully applied lipstick. After a few months of compliance, I found my own songbook: *Torch Songs*. It was full of numbers made famous by Nina Simone, Lena Horne, Sarah Vaughan, and Billie Holiday.

Shirley encouraged me to sing opera, but instead I sang "Black Coffee," "Don't Explain," and "Stormy Weather." For a few months, I actually practiced, squeezed my eyes closed and belted "God Bless the Child" in the shower before school. Somewhere, there is a VHS recording of a recital at our local Unitarian Church, for which I sung "Summertime" (my choice) and Judy Garland's "Smile" (a compromise with Shirley).

I discovered that Billie had been a junkie around the same time I became one. A particularly bad-news boyfriend and I watched Diana Ross's hysterical performance in *Lady Sings the Blues* while nodding out on dope in his Brockton bedroom. A year later, I turned nineteen and moved to New York, hoping I could leave heroin behind, along with that boyfriend. On the wall of my tiny SRO in Chelsea, I tacked a poster of that iconic Billie portrait, first published in *DownBeat* magazine in February 1947. Stage lights illuminate her profile and throw everything else into darkness. The singer's head tilts back as she sings, eyes closed, mouth open, neck tensed yet graceful. Though a simulacrum of pain, there is yielding in her open throat and smooth brow. There was pain in her, yes, but other things, too.

There wasn't a lot of grace in my fight with heroin. But there was a kind of surrender, as there is every time one slides a needle into a vein. Every time, I was not willing to face what feelings existed in me, my vulnerability to the great influx of this life—its vastness of love and hurt and the infinities of other people. The consequences of drugs were known, at least, and I surrendered to their comfort. Though I took great pains to conceal my addiction from everyone who knew me, I naively believed that they would discern my troubles before my troubles killed me. Still, in those early New York days, I kept a packet of razor blades under my mattress, comforted by the promise of that final escape, if I needed it. Junkie belief systems have a capacity for juggling an astounding number of opposing truths at once.

Nights after I drew that needle out of my arm, I dropped the needle on my record player and drew words across notebook pages. Their rhythms rocked my body and pulled something out of me that had no other exit. I chased that other surrender and hoped I could trade one for the other, though I feared the link between them.

As a dope fiend, Billie had known the ease of familiar pains. But she had also surrendered to those songs, to the ribboning moans they pulled from her. She never escaped heroin, but she did leave that haunted voice in whose howl and murmur I heard my own phantoms. I wanted my pain to be worth something, too. Though I could never look at those pages the next morning.

Even at nineteen, my hubris was not so great that I saw much comparison between my and Billie's troubles. She was an African American woman who had been abandoned, raped, arrested, and who came of age in brothels. I was a middle-class child of ambiguous ethnic background who had dropped out of high school, picked up drugs, and become a sex worker. I saw my dark turns as choices. More so than hers, at least. Still, every time I looked at that picture it tugged the part of me to whom her voice had first spoken, before I chose any of that darkness, or it chose me.

In my next apartment, I hung a different poster—an image of Billie's last recording session in 1958, less than a year before her death. She holds a drink and looks decades older than her forty-three years. It is also an image of surrender, but a different kind. She has the vacant pallor that years of addiction give a face. She is dying. A friend of mine

85

once said that it felt wrong to look at her that way. Too intimate. No one should see that much of a person, he meant. But I knew that she wouldn't have cared. The image of that kind of pain is an echo, a dead star's light reaching the eye long after its end.

I was preparing for my own death, studying *my* likely end. I tried to build a story around it that I could live with, or die to. I stopped writing and stopped listening to music. Skinny and silent, I searched the night-sown city, but found only one more ghost-eyed addict to cop for me.

I crouched between the bed and sink of my little room with the phone wedged against my shoulder. *I wish I could tell you what's wrong with me*, I whispered, tears dripping onto my knees. It was a lie and also true.

You can tell me anything, honey, my mother said. After she—or one of my few remaining friends—hung up, I would smoke and stare at that poster of Billie. People had recognized Billie's trouble. She could never conceal it. She was arrested for the last time in her hospital deathbed. I had always identified with her and in those darkest days I also envied her.

Being recognized hadn't saved Billie from death, but it saved me. By some gift of grace or desperation, I found my way to church basements full of people who knew that darkness and had groped their way out. They had words for my unutterables and I listened to them. I surrendered to these

people, to the truth that this world—in all its pain and light—
would not disappear if I hid from it. I needed to remember
this. If I forgot it, nothing else would matter.

The summer I got clean, I carried a photocopied image of
that 1947 photograph into a Lower East Side tattoo shop. I
asked the artist to render it against a solid black rectangle
just above the crook of my arm, where my track marks were
still faintly visible. He began with the outline and filled it in
quickly, a darkening doorway smudged with my blood. After
the first searing minutes, I relaxed and watched Billie's face
emerge from the frame of black ink as if she were rising from
some depth to the surface of my body. When he finished, the
artist swabbed away the blood and ink with a wet cloth and
we both stared down at her in admiration.

As a little girl, my hips and elbows seemed magnetically
attracted to table corners and my forehead never met a car
door it didn't like. My family nickname was Crash. Even
then I chose the familiar consequences of escape. I crashed
into things because I was lost in fantasy or worry or the books
I read even as I walked to the school bus stop.

The thing about pain is that it pins you to the moment, to
your body. People are often surprised that most of my tattoos
came after I got clean, but I didn't need tattoos when I had

heroin. Heroin erases the body. It erases the pain of the moment. It consolidates your troubles in one place: the need to get more heroin. Tattoos helped prepare me for life without heroin—they taught me to hurt without leaving. I discovered that surrendering to the pain lessened it, and let me move through it.

But these scars are also a way of remembering.

When I was a little girl, my father would hold me up to the night sky and name its stars. Head flung back, I squinted at their fiery pinpricks, stunned by my own smallness. The two etched on my left shoulder—Mizar and its orbiting binary, Alcor, sometimes referred to as "horse and rider"—were my favorites. I always searched for that tiny rider, imagined yielding to the pull of such gravity, of possessing it.

The creature that kneels beside those stars has a woman's torso and the flexed neck of a swan, her chin to the ground. Wings arc from her shoulders and bend behind her prostrate form—at once an image of beauty and bondage. Folded forever in this surrender and struggle, she is one of William Blake's "daughters of Albion," an engraving from his prophetic poem "Jerusalem," a figure of thwarted female sexuality, a wish for freedom and a unified self and an oracle foretelling it.

The Virgin Mary who covers my right calf hurt most of all—facedown on the table, I wept onto my arms, the first tears I cried for the death of my abuela, whose name swells beneath that sacred heart.

And the letter *B* on the back of my hip is proof that I have been in love. That what feels permanent rarely is.

As a kid, I used to bury small objects on our property, detail their locations on paper, then hide the maps. No one ever found these objects, but there was satisfaction in their record. When the secret world of my adolescent desires became too much and I could not ask for help, I left my diary in my parents' minivan and was genuinely shocked when they read it. The machinations of my own psyche were still mysterious.

As a young woman, I created another secret world in drugs and desire, and it, too, became a lonely hiding place. Without ever consciously acknowledging my own desire to be seen, I wrote a memoir about that world, a story full of things I'd never spoken aloud to anyone.

It is a violent way to emerge, to tell a secret. There is the delay between the telling and its reaction. The time it takes for someone to lift their eyes from the object onto me. Tattoos are a silent way to say: here are my wounds, my scars, my tender places. We are always doing this anyway, aren't we? We leave clues and hope someone will find them, will care enough to follow. I've never been the type to spill my life story into a stranger's ear. But there are other ways of undressing. In writing, I find the tender spot and start to push, to peel, to name. Then, I send it out into the world—a pretty, throbbing thing; dulled by handling. *Look at me*, I say. *No, look over there, at my image.*

My last breakup before this love showed traces of that blueprint. I still loved that girlfriend, but not the way she needed. I could not speak or even behold the end I had reached. Instead, I gave in to the mouth of my new love, whose touch opened something in me I hadn't known was closed. Then, I wrote about it in my notebook. My girlfriend, for the first and only time, read that account. I brought a flame to the dynamite and plugged my ears. During one of the agonized conversations that followed, she shouted at me, *No one knows you! People love you, but I dare you to let them see all of you.* She was angry and hurt, but not wrong. She saw me perhaps more clearly than anyone has.

It is hard to reveal something you don't understand. These records, then, are for me, too. I manifest my scars tangibly and set down my story in words because I fear that otherwise I could drift through my life like a ghost—driven by unseen motives. I could crash into walls without ever feeling a thing.

She touched my scars. Then she pressed her mouth against every bare place, perhaps wondering where she might mark me. Being reached for is a frightening thing, touch sometimes a painful revelation that one exists. What relief, though, to be seen, even in some small way. It is a gamble on whose odds I bet, however trembling.

The 1947 portrait of Billie, the one I will wear on my body for the rest of my life, is an image of a woman in her cups—an unlovely thing in many ways. It is also an image of opening: her head back, lips parted, throat flexed to the light. She is exposing herself, yes, surrendering to some greater power, but it is no passive act. Her surrender is a fight, and under those lights—that straining neck, those closed eyes, that open mouth—she blazes with it. If these scars are a way of remembering, are the marks of lessons learned, then this scar is a reminder to open. Of the strength it takes. Billie's mouth never closes, and she reminds me to face that light, to bare my blazing throat. Let them see me.

You look pretty, she said, her face in the computer's window a glitter of pixels.

I squinted at my own image in the corner of the Skype screen, and laughed.

What? she asked.

I pointed out that everything I wore—from the wool houndstooth coat to my designer jeans, to my charm-laden necklace and matching gold watch, to my black leather boots and purse, to my underwear and socks—had been gifts from her.

You are a kept woman, she said. *I take good care of you, don't I?*

You do, I agreed, though something clenched inside me.

Well, if we break up, at least you've got a new wardrobe.

If we break up, I said slowly. *Everything you've given me will be ruined, transformed into shrouds of misery.* I smiled.

I don't know about that.

In the time since we met, she had gifted me many things. In this way, she is a generous woman, but especially to those she loves.

It can be difficult to accept the things you want, I've found. Sometimes, it is difficult even to admit them.

We first kissed one night in August after barely speaking and then retreated to our opposite sides of the country: my ocean, her desert. Two weeks later, her first gift arrived.

The "florist" veered around the corner in a Brooklyn delivery van mostly held together by duct tape. He had tracked me down by phone when I didn't answer the doorbell and caught me approaching the C train in Bedford-Stuyvesant. The van screeched up to the curb and he flung the door open to offer me a basket of oranges crowned with a bouquet of matching lilies. On the C, I cradled the basket in my lap and breathed the flowers' musky human scent, quietly swooning as the train shrieked along its track, dragging us under the East River.

I met a friend on the High Line and strolled the landscaped walkway, my arms beginning to ache under their bright burden. As we walked, it caught strangers' eyes—lit first with orange, orange flower, my face, and then the thought: *Someone is falling in love with this woman.*

At the Gagosian Gallery in Chelsea, the reception waif let me stash them under her desk while I watched Richard Phillips's enormous videos of Lindsay Lohan and Sasha

Grey—their towering beauty so radiant, so self-conscious, so crushable I could not look away.

Later, as I searched the far west side for a friend's book party, the heel broke from my shoe. I tucked it into the basket with the oranges, whose glow warmed every alley I tripped down. The party was celebrating a book named after Andromeda. To avoid the awkwardness of arriving with flowers *not* for its author, I hid them in the entryway. As I mingled among partygoers I felt the chain that tied me to them, and to their giver. Like Andromeda, I knew already that fastening in me, but not which of us was rock or goddess or monster or rescue. In the elevator on my way down, I handed out oranges to fellow passengers. They smiled at me, their bright handfuls pulsing—like pieces of stars, of what small blazing thing was growing between us. It had a weight I could feel in my arms, when I hadn't yet felt hers.

The second gift arrived near the end of September. A box of birthday presents, one for every day of that week, each wrapped in a new handkerchief. One day, three slim green notebooks; the next a CD of love songs, their titles listed in her elegant script. The morning of my birthday, the owner of a local bakery hand-delivered a red velvet cake with cream cheese frosting. My favorite.

A week later, she offered me a plane ticket to see her for only the second time. I had never done such a thing—flung myself across the country into a stranger's arms—and I would not have done it without all the small anchors she had cast across the miles between us. Each one tied me to her, to the unlikely story of our love. Each object was a promise, something I could hold when I could barely remember her face. *Stay*, she asked with each one. *Believe in this until you can believe in me.*

Those first gifts were the easiest to receive. We knew so little of what we wanted. We had yet to ask anything from each other but possibility, and thus so little to lose.

My knees shook as I stepped off the plane. I found her waiting in cutoffs, hair falling dark over her shoulders. She stood and looked down at me, still a stranger, and we kissed for the second time. In the hotel, my hands shook as I lifted her shirt over her head and her hair spilled over my arms. Afternoon light shot through the closed blinds in streams, casting shadows across her shoulders, catching the silver scapular whose chain slid around her neck, so long it caught on the dark stars of her nipples.

What's this? she asked about the tattoo on the back of my calf—a Virgin Mary with the word *Abuela* scripted beneath her. My grandmother had been Catholic, I explained, which was why her scapular made such an impression. I'd always loved the paper ones, I said, and she told me of how she'd worn them growing up.

Soon after I returned home, a smaller silver scapular arrived in the mail. I slid that metal thread around my neck, felt the small weight of its pendant against my chest, and pressed my hand over it. I did feel protected, and leaned into the pleasure as I could not have were she watching, were anyone.

I like to be cared for. But I'm uneasy with my desire for it. I fought it for years.

My first long-term boyfriend was a drug addict. I paid for everything. On each of my birthdays that I celebrated with him, I bought *him* an expensive pair of sneakers. It was a sad but safe arrangement. There was no expectation and therefore no disappointment.

In subsequent years, I learned to love people who could pay their own way, if not mine. The first time I remember being consciously disappointed was a birthday in my mid-twenties. That boyfriend, an unemployed graphic designer and anarchist, took me out for a vegan milkshake, and as we rode the train home, I felt a thick, unfamiliar sediment settle in my gut, distinct from the soy cream.

What's wrong? he asked me.

I don't know, I said, a preemptive wave of shame heating my face for what I said next. *It might have been nice to get, like, a little something.*

Like what?

Like a little token of your affection or something. I hated him in that moment, for making me utter this aloud.

Like what, diamonds? We were still in that phase when sneering at privilege amounted to political activism. Couched in this question was his clear judgment against my secret possession of the capitalist values he so loathed.

No, I said. *Not diamonds.*

Five months later, that boyfriend took me out for an Ayurvedic vegan dinner on Valentine's Day. I gave him a button-down from Banana Republic, which he sorely needed for job interviews. He did not give me a gift. We split the bill and outside the restaurant I broke up with him.

I have a friend who'd say that I was shopping for oranges at the hardware store. It's true. It was unreasonable to expect to be showered in gifts by someone I knew to be uniquely unqualified to do so. How often we set this trap for ourselves. I had learned to act as if I were the person I wished to be: an ascetically self-sufficient woman, a woman without needs, a woman immune to disappointment. And I found or urged myself to be attracted to the people whom only such a woman should love.

Partly, this inner conflict was the result of our culture's conflicted relationship to gifts, and to women. I was not indoctrinated in an ideal of feminine dependency by my mother, a Buddhist psychotherapist. Our bookshelves held *The Feminine Mystique*; *Our Bodies, Ourselves*; and *Women Who Run with the Wolves*. I attended feminist marches in my stroller and protested at nuclear power plants during elementary school. I played with blocks on the floor during meetings of our local NOW chapter. My mother revised my children's books with a black Sharpie to render Gretel less dependent on Hansel. In my version, *she* comes up with the breadcrumb strategy. My heroines did not just wait for princes to rescue them, and being loved was not always their goal. But no matter how adamantly my mother boycotted Barbie, she still could not protect me, or herself, from those lessons. I read the issues of *Ms.* that came in our mailbox, but I also coveted glossy issues of *Teen*. I saw women gasp at diamonds in television commercials and collapse into the arms of wealthy men. I still wanted to be a princess, and not for the political power.

When my lover called me a kept woman I felt the tug of this conflict. I wanted to be kept. That is, I wanted a love that felt like belonging. And I had learned as all girls do that material gifts were the easiest proof of this. But I also knew the bait and switch, the way power systems confuse us with shared terminology. That to be "kept" spoke as much of property as affection. Was her femaleness a loophole? I wanted it to be.

My father shipped out to sea for months at a time. There was no Skype. There was no e-mail. There were only letters and they were few and far between. During the rare phone call, his voice piped from so far away it took seconds for his words to reach us. *I love you*, we'd say. And then, *Over*, as if our phone were a walkie-talkie. For a few beats of silence, we waited for our words to cross the ocean. *I love you, too*, we'd finally hear back. And we'd keep waiting.

One year, he was home for my mother's birthday. She made a big deal out of birthdays—baked special cakes, woke us with song, gave gifts that spoke directly to the whims of that particular moment. But on this birthday of hers, he had planned nothing.

Last minute, with no dinner reservation, he took us for a mediocre meal at a mediocre restaurant in town. My mother wept. I was old enough then to diagnose the problem. I learned to hide my wants. I learned to desire in secret.

My lover and I first shopped together at Bloomingdale's. I touched a cashmere sweater, a tailored sheath dress. *Try them on*, she said. *What do you think?* she asked. I knew she meant, *Do you want it?* but I did not know how to say yes. To express a desire for her to buy them for me seemed impossibly vulnerable, and possibly crass.

Giving in to her gifts was a giddy, scary thing. But I got used to it. A delicate gold heart on a hair-thin chain, a tiny ruby embedded in its clasp. A diamond-studded anchor charm. An edition of Carl Jung's illuminated manuscript of *The Red Book*. A pair of Gucci sunglasses. A stack of sand-smoothed stones. Designer purses. A complete *Oxford English Dictionary*. An afternoon's worth of sea-glass shards. Head-to-toe running gear. A gold watch. Massages. Plane tickets. Hotel rooms. Many fine meals.

I could accept these gifts despite that, or maybe because, she failed to give me the one thing I needed: her, undivided. It didn't matter that she claimed to sleep in a separate room from her ex-wife. I never slept. It was too much, but I never said that.

Loving her taught me to be a woman who wants proof of love. Maybe there is no other kind of woman. I struggle to feel loved in my lover's absence. I suffer a kind of emotional object impermanence: out of sight, out of existence. And my beloved was almost always absent. And frequently unavailable. To say that it was painful is an understatement. To say that it was torment is dramatic, but not untrue.

"In many Germanic languages, 'poison' is named by a word equivalent to the English 'gift.'" I heaved open the *OED* she had sent me in the mail and looked it up. I slid the circular magnifying glass down the delicate page and squinted. The entry mentions first, "payment for a wife." It was tempting, during the time that we broke up, to recast her gifts in that unflattering light. As one friend said to me, *You need presence, not presents.* But I always knew that she loved me, that her gifts were an expression of that love, and of the intangibles she could not give, or tell me.

An unromantic, but not contrary way to view it is in terms of exchange. As Marcel Mauss found in his study of archaic societies' gifting conventions (detailed in his seminal anthropological text *The Gift*): gifts are presented as voluntary acts of generosity that actually carry strict obligations for the recipient, both to receive and to reciprocate. Isn't this usually so? At the least, we obligate the recipients of our gifts to reward us with their pleasure and gratitude. Often, we want more than that: love, forgiveness, loyalty, silence, sex, absolution—the gift becomes alms, collateral, bribe, and reward. As Mauss observed: "The obligation attached to a gift itself is not inert. Even when abandoned by the giver, it still forms a part of him. Through it he has a hold over the recipient." Substitute "love" for "gift" and the statement holds. Neither act is wholly unselfish, and perhaps nothing is ever given without hope of some return. I do not think this is a cynical idea. Tenderness does not preclude expectation. And expectation does not preclude tenderness, or generosity.

I wanted to make up the distance, she later told me. My obligation, then, was patience. My obligation was to hold onto these parts of her that had a hold over me. All I had to do was hold onto love in her absence, a task for which I was uniquely unqualified.

My father loved my mother. And he loved me. And he is an exceptionally generous man. But he was a terrible gift-giver, partly due to his absence. A good gift relies on the giver's knowledge of their subject. It answers desires that are only legible under close observation. My father was not there to observe us, and so his gifts were always thoughtful but inaccurate—a complete set of protective pads and a helmet, months after my fleeting infatuation with rollerblading had passed. He returned from sea with exotic treasures for my mother, but gold when she wore silver, big when she wore small. It was never a failure of generosity, but of vision.

My beloved gave good gifts. I don't mean that she gave me beautiful things, though she did. The pleasure of receiving gifts has little to do with their beauty or material value. It is their mirroring. The perfect gift reflects the giver's knowledge of our desires and so carries the precious proof of being known. She was a master of this. Every gift reflected my image in its dazzle and made not only her love but my self more real. Love is so often a wish to have our wants seen and met, without our having to ask.

The heart is a callous repo man. She may not have believed in the capacity of her gifts to become shrouds of misery, but I knew it for fact. One of the most merciless aspects of heart-break is its reaping of love's fruit. Ten months after we met, when my need became too great and she left me, I collected and filled a box with her gifts—the pictures, letters, ticket stubs, stones, jewelry, boarding passes, sea glass, and poems. Even the hand lotion whose scent rung of her disappeared into that box. I learned that the anchor of materialized love has a converse power, too. Just as those objects tethered me to love, to myself, and became a way to close my hand around it, so they gave me something to put away and insisted that I do. I could not bear to look at them. As Mauss claimed, the gift's power is not inert. It carries a part of the giver, as our hearts do. How much easier, sometimes, if we could also put our hearts away. But I could not. I still had my heart when she came back to me, and it still carried a part of her inside it.

My favorite gift was the *wunderkammer*. In Renaissance Europe, "cabinets of curiosities" were all the rage of the ruling classes. Often they were whole rooms populated with treasures and oddities of the natural world: gems and feathers, fossils and taxidermied animals. They were "regarded as a microcosm or theater of the world . . . a memory theater."

On my thirty-third birthday, she presented me with a wooden, glass-lidded box, its interior divided into small compartments. In one of these a corked glass bottle of snake vertebrae. In another, a molded pewter human hand. Every curiosity in the cabinet was a totem, pulsing with meaning. To it, I added the shards of sea glass and the stones.

The best gifts are like these: beautiful and a little grue-some. Such gifts obligate us to see ourselves more fully, to see the many compartments of love, its bones and shards, all its hands and holdings. If the real value of a gift is being known, how can one exclude these darker parts? And it was in loving her that I discovered them.

I need you is both a true and ridiculous thing to say to a beloved. *I would die without you* is never true, though I said it to her, and I meant it. I believed that without her love I would cease to exist. Love is a form of madness, but like all forms of madness, there is logic in its underpinnings, a reason why the melodrama of telenovelas appeals to us, a reason we believe in the value of diamonds. We cannot see ourselves and so depend on the mirror, and sometimes we mistake it for the conjurer. Even in the pixelated window of her vision, I could see myself most clearly. Of course I wanted something to hold onto—I could not hold onto myself.

On our second Valentine's Day, I flew across those 2,500 miles to her. As I descended into her desert, the sky bluer and bigger than it ever is back east, I thought how similar it is to the sea—the wildness, the near infinity of each. I thought of how a wild thing can become known, can become home. I don't remember what she gave me. I only remember the fight we had, her flashing eyes and empty mouth. How I stopped waiting for her to say something I could believe in and simply pressed myself against her.

I delighted in my pretty things, as I worshiped the exquisite aspects of our love, but I still treasure the *wunderkammer*, my memory theater. It reflects more than myself. It is a portrait of its giver, and our love. It is not easy to be seen, no matter how we crave it. It is not easy to look hard at the ones we love. It is always a little gruesome, as love is: full of contradictions and impossible promises. Gift-giving is just a rehearsal. Desires met, a suggestion that it might be safe to need someone. My own need never felt like a pretty thing, though she wanted it. It is a curious thing to give someone. And sometimes a frightening thing to receive. Wanting something does not mean it will suit us.

GIRL AT A WINDOW

The daughter of a captain on the rolling seas
She would stare across the water from the trees
—Jackson Browne, "Jamaica Say You Will"

1

Our first week in Cairo, Egypt, a man grabbed my mother's
ass with both hands. She was hailing a cab in a thunderstorm.
My four-year-old brother clung to her neck while eight-
year-old me clutched her cotton jumpsuit. Rain slapped our
clenched faces.

The Sahara stretched below us and those hot drops
painted the desert red, wilted the men's kaffiyeh scarves like
hibiscus petals around their solemn faces. *American? No,
you are Egyptian!* they said to my brother and me. They
shook their hands at our faces, which were dark as those of
the local children.

It was 1988 and a more liberal Egypt than shortly there-
after or today, but still my mother covered herself from head
to toe. As a woman traveling alone with two children there

was nothing she could do but turn in the pelting rain and meet the gaze of the man whose two hands had clenched her like a sack of corn.

When I think of our weeks in Egypt and the subsequent voyage on the Captain's ship, I think of this moment first. It is so vivid: the rain, my helpless mother, the grip of that stranger's hands. And I do not even remember it. I did not even know that it happened until years later when I was told the story.

The cargo hatches were stuffed with corn. Sacks of it, filling the Captain's ship, the SS *Leslie Lykes*. A steel behemoth two football fields long, with a crew of thirty-six men. She also carried a hatch full of missiles and bombs. After discharging the dangerous cargo in Muscat, Oman, he would steer the *Leslie* north, through the Red Sea and Suez Canal, to meet us in Alexandria.

We had not seen him in four months. Our arms were still sore from vaccinations. We dropped our beloved dog off at a friend's house and flew out of Boston at dinnertime. It was winter and already dark.

As we began our descent into Paris early the next morning, my brother had only just fallen asleep—his dark lashes fluttering in the dim cabin lights. My mother took us each by hand as we debarked the plane and moved into the airport, blinking at its scrim of cigarette smoke and illegible syllables. He began to cry. He cried so hard that she had to carry him as she navigated the foreign signage. *You?* she tells me. *You were yourself. You were fine.*

There was a clear before and after, my mother explains when I first ask her about our time abroad. The before consisted of us three waiting for the ship to reach port in Alexandria. We landed at the Cairo airport—*like a cinderblock in the middle of the desert*—all the flight's luggage dumped in a massive pile on the asphalt, swarmed by eager men, *Lady I help you lady I help you lady I help you.*

The *Leslie* was scheduled to reach Alexandria a week after we arrived in Cairo. My mother was supposed to call the Captain's agent to coordinate our travel there. A hotel employee helped her use the phone. The number he had given her was dead.

It was terrible, she tells me. *I had no one to help me. Two little kids, all our luggage, and I couldn't even read the signs.* But after a few days more in Cairo, she got us to Alexandria. She checked us into a hotel and prayed he would find us. *We had no way of knowing if the ship was delayed*, she tells me. It was delayed for nearly a week.

My mother's father abandoned them when she was four. My grandmother supported her two daughters working as a secretary at Rutgers and doing typing for academics on the side. During summer breaks my mother lived for stints with relatives in nearby towns. She cooked herself dinners at five years old. She developed the mix of self-sufficiency and hunger for romance that I have come to recognize in myself.

I loved my mother's story as I loved my fairy tales. It had suffering and a happy ending. *I always wanted a baby girl,* she told me. *And then you came.* My mother wanted to be a different kind of parent. She wanted a husband who wouldn't leave. She wanted love to heal the wounds of her past.

Eyes always widened when I told people that my father was a sea captain. *Do those still exist?* they asked. The time of sea captains had passed. The industry of sea merchants is now even further gone. That work has been outsourced and replaced. The lives that once existed in its orbit, of which we were among the last, are relegated to romantic history.

A century before us, the wives of Nantucket and Cape Cod whalers lived in close-knit communities on the same land. They were their husbands' true partners. They managed finances, ran households, raised children, and operated within a woman-run home economy of traded services and goods. The sea wife was, in the words of novelist Amy Brill, "a sun-weathered, calloused, shrewd business-woman with intellectual and physical desires on par with her seagoing husband." Both written evidence and artifact attest to the popularity of the "he's-at-home," an early ceramic dildo. Instead of a recurrent abandonment, this absence of husbands seems a grant of freedom comparable to the entrance of women to industrial fields during World War II.

My mother had no bustling network of fellow sea wives. She was alone in her experience, isolated with two young children in a rural area far from the place she had grown up. She only had us. And she did not own a dildo. I would have come across it in my occasional snooping through her bedroom. I did find letters from the Captain in her jewelry box. His tidy script covered opaque pages with descriptions of the things he saw overseas and the minor dramas among crewmen. He asked about us and told her he loved her. These letters disappointed me. I suspect her as well. The only news we wanted was of his return.

The life of a sea captain's wife is lonely. My mother must have known this when she married him. But the loneliness she had known before him was of a different kind. The Captain would take care of us.

But what does it mean to be taken care of? Material security. Adoration. Until we obtain these, they seem the objects of our desire. But these concepts of care are false fronts. They are colorful screens we rip through as soon as we reach them. We really want the undoing of our earliest wounds and sometimes, in our attempts to correct the errors of our childhoods, we choose the exact thing we hope to avoid. We recognize a chance for love's redemption and run toward it. We hope for a different ending.

The Captain has an accurate but selective memory. When I ask him about those first weeks in Egypt he does not mention the dead phone number. His memories of that time barely overlap with my mother's, though they are even richer in detail. He recounts our trip to the ancient city of Luxor. *Eighty-thousand slaves*, he tells me, *lived in Luxor to support and keep rebuilding that holy city for the gods.* He bought us tickets to a sound and light show and we walked through Luxor's enormous stone buildings: 110-foot high walls and gates, statues of pharaohs and beasts, every object there four to six thousand years old. The show ended in a stone amphitheater with an enormous reflecting pool in which we saw the stars, whose names he had already taught me.

My abuelo didn't abandon his family. But they would have been better off if he had. He crashed cars. He passed out with his face in full plates of *arroz con pollo*. When my youngest uncle, at the age of six, asked my abuelo why he didn't stop drinking, my abuelo began to choke him. My father, his older brother, and my abuela leapt onto him like furious *satos*, screaming for him to stop. They feared he might kill his youngest son, and perhaps he would have.

While he waited to grow big enough to fight his father, the Captain did his homework. He became a Life Scout. He went to church. He won wrestling matches and graduated from the Maritime Academy. He became a leader and a follower of rules. There was a right way to do everything on ships. It was a life that made sense. It was a solution to the chaos from which he came and the ways it still tormented him.

The Captain had also dreamed of being a parent, of fatherhood as a way to correct the crimes of his own father. We listened to the terrible parables of his childhood and understood that we, his children and wife, would never suffer that way.

Toward the end of many three-month voyages, he would call my mother and tell her he had accepted another assignment. *Two more months*. Sometimes, he'd call again after the two months were up. *One more month*. At thirty-three (my age, when I began writing this essay), he would be among the youngest captains in the company's history and one of only two Puerto Rican ones.

A uniform changes a man. The first week after his returns he seemed more captain than father. Once when he returned with a beard, I sobbed, unable to recognize him. Then, he would soften. He wrote me songs on his guitar, read bedtime stories, and coached our baseball teams. Then, he'd leave again. As time passed, it was not so much he who changed at sea but we who changed back home. It no longer seemed worth telling him about my favorite books. By the time he understood the new landscape of my interests, he was gone again.

The Captain never spoke directly to us about what his job meant. Maybe we would not have understood if he had. I don't know if he ever explained to my mother exactly how he needed the sea and the self he became upon it. Maybe he didn't have those words. No one explained to us that marriage was an agreement they'd made, that each of their expectations had been disappointed. All we knew was our empty home. Our mother's despair.

If he loved us, if he really loved us, where was he?

I loved Salvador Dalí's surrealist landscapes as a teenager. My favorite painting was his most realist, "Girl at a Window," which features a woman with her elbows resting on an open window's sill as she stares out over a bay. The image described both my actual experience of a life characterized by waiting and the romantic vision of the sea wife, which, as I aged, offered some comfort, too. A sea daughter is also a kind of Penelope. My tendency toward nautical and sea images as an adult writer reflects this same dialectic attachment: to my real experience and to the romance that softened it. It is a quality the Captain and I share. We build theaters of our memories, and in that partial darkness we find a story that makes sense of their pain.

The easiest stories to romanticize were the ones he brought back from sea. *Tell us about when you broke Bill Skye out of the Algerian prison!* we demanded. The Captain's brow lowered. *That was not a good time.* But we knew that he didn't mind telling us the story. It had a good ending. *Tell us about the pirates!* we begged. And again his face darkened. *Pirates are not what you see in the movies,* he'd remind us. We already knew. Cartoonish renditions of sea robbers offended him nearly as much as

Catholic Bible interpretations. They were both dangerous fairy tales.

In 1987, the Captain was First Mate on the SS *Allison Lykes*. Recent pirate attacks on merchant liners had his crew of 36 alert as they ran the west coast of South America and dropped the hook five miles outside Guayaquil, Ecuador. Shortly before dawn the next morning, forty men in canoes flung their grappling hooks over the deck and climbed aboard, machetes dangling from their belts.

The *Allison's* crew had only radios and the element of surprise to their advantage. The Captain led the deck department of fifteen men in an attack armed only with two flare guns, a shotgun holding blank shells, pipe stanchions, and steel cones. They rushed the pirates, screaming and hurling steel. The ship's whistle blared and flares glowed the dark red. The pirates panicked and jumped overboard. Only a few pools of crimson blood on the deck remained after they fled in their canoes.

The story was meant to impose upon us the gravity of real danger and puncture the silly image of bearded villains with hooks for hands. It still dazzled. The Captain was a magnificent storyteller. He was a real-life hero. I think he appreciated these stories as much as we did—however perilous, his troubles at sea were simpler than those at home, and his role in them was always clear.

What is a ship but a small steel world over which my captain was king? My mother was a land whose laws defied him.

My mother barely mentions the Valley of the Kings when I ask about our time in Egypt. She better remembers the cab driver who ferried us all around Alexandria—Farouck. *He was very young,* she tells me. *Very cute.*

My mother rarely wore makeup and never painted her nails or wore heels. It didn't matter. Men stared at her everywhere. They flirted with her from behind counters and tollbooth windows. College boyfriends still called on her birthday. She didn't court this attention, but I don't think she minded it. I know the power of being wanted. It is balm for the fear of being left.

She went alone one day to visit a site that none of us were interested in. *I felt so grown up,* she tells me. *And I was so young. Thirty-three. Your age.* The cabby charmed her. *He was funny,* she says. *I thought, what if I just lived here and married this cabby?* Her voice grows lighter. *I do that whenever I travel. Just think, what would it be like to live here and marry a local cabby?* We both laugh. *Do you know what I mean?* she asks. I do.

I also wonder. I have peered into the orange-lit apartment windows on the train ride home through my city. In foreign cities. I have fallen in momentary love with strangers. Maybe it is simple curiosity. Maybe it is a symptom of disappointment or fear of disappointment. A hope that somewhere else might be the truer life or love you have hoped for.

My mother relates to the world through a permeable membrane. She can imagine herself in a different life and has recast herself many times. As I have. It is a way to move through the world driven equally by hope and fear. We who fear abandonment are often the most capable of leaving. We build lives out of moveable pieces. Out of ourselves. It is a creative way to live, both variable and resilient, if sometimes lonely. The Captain built a life out of systems and stories that featured him in a fixed role: captain, hero, father, husband. He would not have left my mother for the same reason he could not leave his ship: he would have lost himself.

My mother burst into tears as the Captain's agent strode through the hotel lobby in Alexandria. *We were taken care of after he found us,* she says. The ship arrived two days later. *I hadn't seen him in months* is all she says of their reunion.

The Captain spun her around the kitchen when he was home. *Look how beautiful your mother is!* She blushed happily and so did we. He worshiped her. Worship is a tricky gift. It is a love meant for gods, not humans. We idolize our objects of worship and no human can meet those expectations.

I woke one night and listened to them fight in the room above mine. He had just returned home after months at sea. They shouted in pitches I'd never heard and the sounds tore from their mouths. I sat up in my bed. The ceiling thudded as if something heavy had fallen or been thrown. They soon came downstairs to my room to explain. They did not tell me that my mother had slept with another man. They did not tell me that this was not what either of them had expected.

After the affair, we moved to a different Cape Cod town. From the harbor of our new town we could see the murky scrawls of Nantucket and Martha's Vineyard against the horizon. They agreed on a new story: they were starting over. And the voyage was a part of it.

We left Alexandria and saw the winding *souks* of the *casbah* in Tangier. We drank sweet mint tea out of gleaming samovars and ate decadent pressed nougat. We sailed through the

Strait of Gibraltar to Casablanca. We passed the volcanic cone of Madeira Island and porpoises and flying fish leapt in our wake at its foot. The ship's bosun built my brother and me a "sandbox" filled with loose corn from the cargo holds. I played cards every morning in the mess hall with Rosemary, the Chief Engineer's wife and only other woman on the ship besides my mother.

While we waited for the *Leslie*, we spent three days at the pyramids of Giza. Then, the Great Sphinx. My mother still has one of the photographs on her mantel. She holds my brother in her lap and the pyramids sprawl behind them like a photo backdrop at a state fair. Though my brother remembers the basement smell of the pyramid's inner tomb better than any other detail of the trip, they are just stories to me now, corroborated by the plastic baggie of crumbled stone (circa 2560 B.C.) that my mother collected from the base of the Great Pyramid.

When *I* think of those months abroad, I think of those early days in Cairo. I think of my mother alone. Waiting.

The work of love is in building a shared story, and in letting the differences in perception rest easily aside one another. My parents couldn't do it. In the story of our voyage, the Captain remembers the happy parts. My mother remembers the hard.

I understood early that love was a mission to heal one's own heart. We are attracted to the people who can open our wounds. And lovers want their healing to also be love's happy ending. But our healing is never dependent on love's success. Sometimes you have to break your own heart to mend it.

A year after we returned home, my parents sat us down in our living room and told us they were separating.

2

In the years after they separated, the Captain often accused me of borrowing my mother's perspective. In one fight during my adolescent years I said that he had abandoned us. He glowered at me. *That's your mother talking*, he said.

I kept a diary at twelve years old. In the early years after my body's abrupt transformation, it functioned as a catalog of the men I let touch me. Frankie. Tony. Shawn. Tammy's cousin. Tammy's cousin's friend. First base. Second base. Third base. I told no one but that book.

There were no words for *why*. Their hands lifted me out of something. They touched me and I didn't fear being left. I didn't think of anything. It seemed that I could compel the attention of any older man. I did not connect this fleeting empowerment to the Captain's leaving and my own failure to compel him near until much later. It did not occur to him, either, when he read that diary.

How could you? he asked me. I had no answer. I could not look at him. I could not bear being seen. But it still hurt when he stopped looking. Though a clumsy child, I was a scrupulous keeper of secrets. And I had left my diary on the floor of his car.

Fear of abandonment begets abandonment. I gave myself away to solve the pain of his leaving and in doing so performed my own abandonment. The Captain stepped away from that hurt. And on we went.

I shaved my head. I dropped out of high school. I moved out at two weeks shy of my seventeenth birthday. All of it confounded him. Frustrated him. It is difficult to be so perfectly hurt and not feel it was intended. And I was only getting started.

One job description for a professional dominatrix is to be worshiped. For three years, men paid to press their cheeks against my feet. They pleaded to smell my armpits. They bowed their foreheads to the floor and begged for my touch.

They wanted my violence and tenderness in equal amounts. They craved my fury. They wanted schoolgirl uniforms and baby talk. They wanted mean teenager. These were splintered pieces that for a time felt like everything.

I have also been worshiped by lovers. I craved that glazed gaze of the lovesick. The dreamy focus of lovers squinting through their own reflection. Worship intoxicates probably because it mimics parental love. And this is the love we are socialized to seek. The worshipper projects perfection onto their beloved as a parent does his child. To both the child and the beloved this worship feels complete. It feels like the safety we long for. For the child it often is. But what feels unconditional to the beloved is far from it. To be seen as perfect makes you feel perfect. And for people like my mother and me, whose psyches are ever preoccupied with the danger of being abandoned, it has a loud call. But it is a source of self-esteem wholly dependent on the external mirror of the lover.

I'll take care of you, they say. *I would do anything for you. I would die without you.* What other promises did my mother hear? *I will take you places. I will always love you.* They are always the magic words, the ones we most crave to hear.

Worship is the white whale. The thing we believe will fill our heart's belly for good. Nothing can. And the ones we most believe in are the ones that break us. Worship always begets mutual betrayal. The worshipful lover is Pygmalion— the woman he loves is his own creation. And when she proves to be someone other than this she becomes his Eliza Doolittle. My mother may never forgive the Captain for failing to take care of her, and he may never forgive her for breaking the mold.

He was relentless, my mother said. The husband of our neighbor. *Your father was always gone.* I nodded. *I was so alone.* She couldn't see me in my bedroom in Brooklyn with the phone cord wrapped around my fingers. My head ached. My hands damp. I had spent the weekend shooting heroin. I had always seen her as Penelope. The faithful wife, long-suffering, abandoned by her husband for his personal glory. My story flickered as its parts shifted. *I just gave in*, she said.

In the days that we waited for the Captain in Egypt, my mother took us to a papyrus museum. The aquatic and flowering *Cyperus papyrus* was most known for its paper. It was also used to make boats. Sailors wove its strong reeds into sails, mats, and rope.

My schoolteachers had sent me abroad with a small blue notebook. I was supposed to record accounts of my adventures in it. A child's log book.

In the papyrus museum gift shop my mother purchased a scroll bearing an inked prayer. Twenty-five years later, it is rolled in her attic amid our childhood drawings and tiny shoes. She has forgotten its meaning. I imagine her prayers in those days—*God, bring him home. God, take care of my children. God, let it all work out.* Every prayer is answered, I think, though not often in the ways we imagine.

I left the world of worship and quit heroin. Then I wrote a book about it. It was still a conversation that I only knew how to have on paper. It was the best way I found to understand it. To be less alone in it.

To my surprise, the scene in the book that most hurt the Captain does not take place in the dungeon. It recounts a brunch I shared with him and my abuela. He remembered this brunch as a hallmark in the renaissance of our relationship. The book revealed to him that the night previous I had relapsed on a drug binge. I had faked my way through the meal. Numb and ravaged, I chattered about college and pushed my food around my plate. I vomited in a public trashcan after they left. I had squashed my despair and congratulated myself for having maintained my façade of precocious daughter and granddaughter.

The Captain had been so proud of our closeness and his righting of the wrongs done him as a son. My book robbed him of that. We did not speak for three months after I sent him the manuscript. In our first conversation he compared my memoir to a pie in the face. *I can't believe how wrong I was about our relationship*, he said. *About who I am as a father*. His brow furrowed in dismay and anger.

The book wasn't about you, I said. *It was about me.* I still did not know how to explain that I had made those choices out of self-preservation. To avoid hurt instead of provoke it.

The Captain still loves my mother. And he may never forgive her betrayal. She destroyed his story of their marriage. Or revealed the ways in which it was already broken.

I was indignant when he accused me of borrowing my mother's words. Now I can see that he was right. My mother's and my experience overlapped in principle ways and I identified more with her version of their story. How could I not? She was the one I relied on all those years. I was privy to her story as it unfolded. I knew it was true.

Today I know that my Captain's story was also true. But he was halfway across the world when he lived it. He told us the stories of his childhood and he told us his stories of the sea. He never explained how these parts of him were connected.

We are more alike than I ever thought. My stories are containers into which I pour myself and the indigestible parts of my experience. In them, I become a woman who can look at things. Who knows what to do next and how. A ship is also a story.

My father and I both still need our containers. Once filled, they carry more of us than our lovers can bear, than we can. And sometimes they carry us away. I wonder if he has learned, as I have, how the things that save us can cost us.

I know this with absolute certainty: If a beloved asked me to choose between her and the story my life is built upon, I would likely make the same choice he did.

Three years after my book's publication, he and I spent a weekend in a cabin on the beach of the Quileute Indian Reservation—La Push—the furthest northwest point of this country. He brought his guitar and I brought my notebooks. He played the songs that he'd sung me as a child. I had never noticed how apt these anthems were. James Taylor's "Sweet Baby James," which tells of *a song that they sing when they take to the highway / a song that they sing when they take to the sea*. Jackson Browne's "Jamaica Say You Will," a love song to *the daughter of a captain on the rolling seas*.

On our last morning I went for a run by the water. Great antlers of driftwood lay scattered across the beach. I thought about our story as waves lapped that dark sand.

The Captain loves to tell people how as a toddler, with a book opened in my tiny hands, I would back into the knees of anyone sitting and command, *Wead!* He repeated my favorite stories with endless patience. *The Story of Ferdinand. Frog and Toad. The Lone Ranger* for the duration of a six-hour car trip, until my mother couldn't take it anymore.

Children learn through repetition. They appreciate the predictable. But I don't think I will be the kind of parent who can share in that pleasure, not like the Captain did. Few can. He still delights in stories that are all hero and rescue and happy ending. From him, I learned my love for the movies, the glory of telling well a very long joke, and that our life was a happy ending to the hard story of his childhood. But when my story departed from his, I ruined his happy ending. In this way, perhaps every father is a Pygmalion.

I returned to our cabin and asked him to sit down.

I'm sorry, I told him. *I'm so sorry that I hurt you.* I listed the ways I knew I had. The Captain, my true father, with his kind face and curly hair, thanked me. He shook his head. *It hurt so much*, he said. *I had thought we were close. I thought I'd been a good father to you.* He frowned. *It felt like you did it to hurt me.*

I didn't, I said.

He nodded. His face creased deeper.

My father was a monster, he said. *We warned you both about drinking, about drugs. We tried to do everything right. And it didn't work.* He stood and walked to the sink. He began washing our breakfast dishes. He spoke more about his own father. I listened to the stories I had heard so many years before and I finally understood. He had looked at me and seen his own ghosts. His own failure. He hadn't blamed me for hurting myself. He had blamed me for the death of his story.

He scrubbed and spoke and I watched the scissor of his arms in their flannel shirt. I stood up and went to him. I wrapped my arms around his waist and lay my cheek against the soft back of his shirt. He went quiet. He stopped washing and folded his hands over my hands.

Since then, we have made some peace over the differences between our stories. He asked me to check with him before

I publish anything that concerns events that he might remember. *I can't promise you that*, I said. Maybe he understood. As time passes, he seems more able to accept that my memories don't erase his. They are simply different. And I have become able to cherish his stories as I did when I was a little girl.

I used to think of our family's voyage as my parents' last effort to save their marriage. But it was much more than that. It was the last chapter of our family together. It was extraordinary. Maybe it has been easier all these years to look at the hard parts because they make sense of our ending. When I remember the good, I must remember how it broke my heart to lose it. But it is worth it to remember how fiercely I was loved and all that I was given. My Captain, my father, teller of bedtime stories and singer of songs, he taught me this. Of our story, I wouldn't change a thing.

When he reads this he will blanch at my inaccuracies. And it's true that his memory is better than mine. It can't be easy to have a daughter who is a writer. But there is no one true version of any story. Some parts we share and some are ours alone. Here is mine. And there is my family, waving from the shore.

And if longing seizes you for sailing the stormy seas,
when the Pleiades flee mighty Orion
and plunge into the misty deep
and all the gusty winds are raging,
then do not keep your ship on the wine-dark sea
but, as I bid you, remember to work the land.

—Hesiod, *Works and Days*

1

Every story begins with an unraveling. This story starts with a kiss. Her mouth the soft nail on which my life snagged, and tore open.

That afternoon, we swam together in a lake named Pleiad. My father, the Captain, had pointed out this constellation to me as a little girl. Formed over one hundred million years, it is the star cluster most visible to the human eye, and its name derives from the Greek πλεῖν, "to sail" because seamen relied on it, as "the season of navigation began with their heliacal rising."

The seven sisters were daughters of Atlas and hand-maidens to the huntress Artemis. In one story, after their father is sentenced to carry the heavens, they kill themselves out of grief. Zeus transforms them into stars—*catasterism*—to immortalize them. Other stories tell of Orion's desirous pursuit of the sisters, and Zeus's catasterism as a rescue. We call them the seven sisters, though only six are visible. Merope, the youngest sister, fell in love with the hunter.

Near the end of an academic conference, four of us followed a trail across the shoulder of a mountain to this rock bowl filled with water. We were not sisters, but strangers. No horny Orion chased us through those woods, or across the sky. I just drove us up the mountain and parked under some trees. Something was chasing me, though, some mad hunter, my own hot heart. I was out of love with someone, out of my mind in that coldest, most sane, most lonely way. I didn't want to go home.

When I'd left New York ten days earlier, I'd decided not to cheat. It was an exit I'd used before and didn't want to again. I closed a door in me and it worked. At the lake, I did not want her, but I noticed that long body when she peeled off her clothes on the ridge of that rock. Seeing her neck for the first time, I wondered how it would feel under my tongue, about the taste of that neck. Just curious.

Hair seal-black and slick, she watched me from the water. Eyes dark embers, hands slender rudders, turning. I did not notice her hands: long fingers pulling her T-shirt over those broad shoulders, touching the water as she waded into it. I did not imagine her fingers closed around my throat, my hip, my wrists; driving inside me deeper than words, leaving me dumb, mouth hung open, eyes wet, body shaking stupid and soft.

I didn't mean to lose myself. And I never planned to find my father. Of all the things that happened in the two years after that swim, the only thing that felt like a choice was her. I must have known that she could lead me to it all.

When did I decide? Not at the lake. Not on the drive back down the mountain. That night. In a crowded bar, she leaned over me, hair silking against my bare shoulder. She hooked one finger through my belt loop and pulled my hips' string, and they wound—they touched hers and kept going. I must have known then that I could leave it up to her. That she would insist.

I have to go, I said. *I cannot kiss your mouth*, I meant. *I cannot stop my hips this rocking toward you.* She nodded. I did not go. I closed my hand around her knee, and bared my teeth. A smile is a grimace is a yielding is a glimpse inside—the mouth's soft muscles, opening. *Help me*, I thought.

Those few moments before our mouths met: faces touching, breath everywhere as our bodies tipped, hands soft with giving in, mouths even softer.

In the shower before sleep, I soaped between my legs—so swollen and wet, it shocked me. I could not wash it away. Under the hot water, I traced the life I had left in New York: the home I was headed back to, the woman who loved and needed me. I tried to remember the solid thing I'd been only hours before. It was already blurry. It was dissolving like a dream from which I'd just woken.

The next morning, she wrote me: *What was that poem about "the face that launch'd a thousand ships"? And burnt "the topless towers of Ilium"? I can't remember, but like that kiss, yours took something from me, or gave me something. I'll never stop thinking of it.*

I knew almost nothing about her, only that she was of Chilean descent—part indigenous, part Spanish—and had the gravity of a planet. She occupied her body and the space she moved through with a certainty I suddenly did not feel in myself. She was an anchor, and I, Andromeda, I tied myself to her that night. Not in the usual way.

2

The next day, I met my half sister for the first time. I felt no mounted tension, just an impulse, a tug in a certain direction that I heeded. I had known for two years that my half sister lived in Vermont. She knew about me, too. We had never met, but after that swim in the lake, I wrote to my sister—*I am passing through. Can I see you?*

My adoptive father, the sea captain, always encouraged me to find my siblings. *Just think*, he'd say, *there's people out there who look like you!* He never encouraged me to reunite with Jon, my biological father whom I'd met only once. But I didn't wonder—my connection to Jon was scientific, a quirk of nature's mechanics.

Though we are not biologically related, the Captain and I look alike. My (half) brother and I look strikingly alike. The older I get, the more my mother's face emerges in the mirror.

But I had never seen a mouth like mine. I have always noticed strangers with green eyes and olive skin, felt a recognition pass between us. We are estranged members of the same tribe. Everyone recognizes their small ears on the bank teller, their wide feet in the locker room, their hips switching across the street. Don't they?

I passed through hours of farmland with little to see but gleaming grain elevators and murky creeks scrawled along the roadside. The sun blazed. My body buzzed and sweated. For a few minutes, a bee hovered inside the car, beating gently against the windshield until she found my open window.

My half sister lives in a suburb of Burlington that looks rich. It looks like the housing developments that have crept through the rural Cape Cod neighborhood where I grew up, replacing the woods that I roamed as a child. The homes are big and similar; the lawns green; the children all white and watched by women close behind them. I cruised by the country club she had chosen for our meeting and parked in the lot of the church across the street.

I didn't want to walk into that country club restaurant. I wanted to walk into the cool empty church and close my eyes for a long time. My mind circled for twenty minutes, beating gently against the windshield, my sister, my buzzing body, my home an egg I'd cracked on the lip of that kiss. I listened to one song over and over. *Ha ha ha ha Armageddon*, the singer screamed. *Ha ha ha ha Armageddon.*

I turned up the air conditioner and pressed my hands into my thighs. There were sweat stains under my arms and shadows under my eyes. My heart thrummed. I did not know what I should be feeling. I was in that parking lot, seeking out a woman to whom I did not feel connected. The previous night, I had resisted a woman to whom I felt irresistibly drawn, and failed.

A sliver of fear turned in me, its tiny blade the scraping thought that I had engineered this meeting. I had brought us here. I would lead the conversation. I would judge the success or failure of our meeting. And then, I would go home to break a heart that I loved. How can I explain this? It was the fear of no God. The fear that I was following a stranger through my life, and that stranger was me.

The cold inside the restaurant relieved me, and justified the cardigan I'd worn to hide my tattoos and sweat stains. In the restaurant bathroom, however, I found a stain on the front. An old feeling foamed in me: I am too messy for places like this. I am too dark. My body is too obvious. Places like this, where skinny white women lunch, have always made me feel like a swollen thing, uncouth and over-sexual, too animal. In the bathroom mirror I saw my nipples hard under the stained sweater, and a halo of frizz encircling my face—mouth swollen, eyes sunken. In the bathroom stall, I pressed a damp hand against my chest and felt my own breath.

Half sister. It means that we share 25 percent of our DNA. Half sister is a halved paper doll. An exquisite corpse of a girl—those drawings we did as children: draw half a body, fold the paper, pass it, and let the other person draw the other half blind. She is sister to the half of me beyond the folded edge. Perhaps the shadow half, from which my dark urges spring, these clutching unscrupulous parts that belong to neither of the parents who raised me, this want to drink and smoke and shoot and fuck and puke and weep until the skin peels from my face, to fling myself at hard edges until the life shakes out of my body. I know these drives, but not from where they come.

I wondered if in her I might find or awaken that lost part. If I have been living in only one half of me all these years, I thought, then God help me should I ever discover the other half.

3

Here are the things I knew about my birth father:

- His name was Jon.
- He was a career drug addict and alcoholic.
- He was Wampanoag.
- He played guitar.
- He had other children.
- He raised none of us.

I was a curious child but I was never curious about Jon. Jon was just Jon. He was a fact the size of a postage stamp, which my mother once wryly suggested he had never in his life purchased.

Jon was not a mystery. Jon was a small suitcase that my parents unpacked for me as a child. *See?* they said. *Here is what he left you.* The neat circular vowels of *biological* and *Wampanoag*, the empty bottle with the skull and crossbones on its label, and the endless double helical strands of 50 percent of my DNA, glimmering coils as perfect as the skin of an apple peeled by my mother's knife.

Not much to see here, they shrugged. *But it's yours.* I ran my fingers along the tops of those letters, felt the spine of the little *b*, the *l*'s, and the *w*. I looked through the glass bottle, my parents' faces rippled on the other side. I repacked the suitcase and put it on the closet shelf. Over the years my mother warned me about the drinking. *It's hereditary*, she told me. But little else was assigned to that half of my blueprint. *You probably don't have much in common with them,* she said of my unknown half siblings.

Then, when I was eight, I started eating my pancakes with butter and salt instead of maple syrup. The first time I reached for the saltshaker, my mother froze.

Jon used to eat his pancakes with butter and salt, she said, not in her usual voice, but slower, her mouth turning the words like prickly lozenges.

I put that saltshaker in the suitcase, too, but didn't forget it like the other things.

When I was still a baby, my mother packed all our belongings in her car, and we left this gentle mess of a man. Two years later, she married a handsome Puerto Rican sea captain.

The Captain adopted me when he married my mother, but I never felt adopted. I was still raised by my biological mother. And the Captain felt like my father. My new birth certificate bore his name. Our faces bore resemblance. We are both much browner than my pale mother. We are both athletic. We were both born without the same tooth: our second incisors. We loved each other unreservedly.

In my twenties, just after I'd kicked heroin but before I learned to feed myself, when I was still working as a professional dominatrix, I told a therapist that I often forgot the Captain was not my biological father. I told her that I had never been curious about Jon, that I often forgot he existed at all. That, she said, was the mark of a successful adoption.

4

I returned to the empty restaurant's bar. My sister was waiting. I recognized her by her nervousness, but she is a lady who lunches at such places. She is blonde and pretty, her body fit and modest. If we were two halves, *I* was the darker one. Maybe I should have been comforted to find this tidier half. Of course, no one is one of those ladies who lunches. We are all animal, all these fearing, sleeping, shitting beings. I was her exquisite corpse, too, and while I couldn't say what lay beyond her fold, I saw her peering around that bend, to see where I was coming from, and if it looked familiar.

You have a younger brother? I asked, though I had already found a picture of his face and seen the resemblance to mine.

Sort of, she said. *He's not*, she paused. *Curious about you. The way that I am.*

I nodded.

You have kids? I asked.

Two boys and a girl, she said. They were campers and skiers. The husband in business.

Symmetries emerged. We both have replacement fathers and a bruised quality I could see under the patina of her prettiness, her nice life, her manners. She ate her bunless burger and I my salad, so careful not to splatter vinegar on my already stained sweater.

I work at a college, I said. *I'm a professor.* I did not mention the memoir I'd written about when I worked as a dominatrix. I did not mention my girlfriend.

I imagined kissing her. It did not surprise me. I must always glimpse the worst thing, the thing I must not do. The worst thing is so often sexual. That jolt of shock, as the phantom self steps forward and does it. A shard of time in which I cannot be sure if I have done it or not—quick and convincing as the waking moment before the dream and the real are teased apart. Staring over the edge of a city rooftop, suddenly afraid I must jump, that to even contemplate such a thing might mean yielding to the part of me that would do it.

I imagined kissing her as a test. If she were my sister, my real sister, if *sister* really meant something, if biology meant something, wouldn't I feel magnetically repelled by the thought of kissing her? It was a cracked hypothesis. I didn't want to kiss her, but it proved nothing.

Toward the end of our meal, I ran out of questions and realized how few she'd asked me.

I read your book, she said, finally. And then I knew: she had all the answers. She knew everything that one would never think to tell a stranger. She knew the things I'd done that I still cannot say aloud.

You did?

Of course.

I knew also, then, that she had seen all the rest. At that time there was little of my external life not available on the Internet.

How is your partner's health? she asked, and I blanched inside.

She's better, I said, though she had been doing very poorly the whole time I'd been at the conference and would soon be doing poorly in a wholly different way.

We stared at each other then, over our empty plates, and something parted. Or rose up in each of us enough for the other to see. It started with shame. Not the word, or any I could have named in those moments, but the fizz of embarrassment that she could see me—my queerness of so many kinds, my unwieldy body, my life an open chest of drawers whose dirty things spilled out.

I don't know what she saw across the table, but when I looked up at her, she looked down at her plate. Her forehead creased, and that bruised part of her flashed its purple back, and I saw not my own reflection, but that same shame in her.

We don't know any artists, she said, pinching her napkin with two manicured fingers. *I'm just a mom. I've never even been to New York.*

Before I drove away, she stood outside my car's open window and squinted into the humming afternoon. We agreed to stay in touch but both knew we might not. In those last moments something had loosened, or been loosed. When she met my eyes, I felt it move between us.

I've always wanted a sister, she said. And then she smiled. I smiled back, both of us shy but wry in our knowing how little that word, or any, could name us.

5

The first time Amaia and I spoke on the phone was a Sunday. I sat in my apartment, which had just been emptied of everything but sunlight. My ex had left a single fork and mug in the sink. I was waiting for the new bed to be delivered. I had a one-word list of things I needed: *everything*.

Years earlier, as part of the Twelve Steps, I wrote a list of all the people against whom I held resentments. I wrote a list of all the people I had ever harmed. I wrote a list of all the things I wanted in a partner. *Someone with tools*, I had written. *A good communicator. Trustworthy. Physically and emotionally available.*

I had seen my own part in those resentments and they had been lifted. I had made amends to all the people I had harmed. It is easier to have insight about the past, when you decide to look at it. A list of the future is just a wish.

On the counter sat a vase of flowers that Amaia had sent me. She had also sent a birthday cake, a CD of love songs, three green notebooks, a pack of strawberry Mentos (the candy she'd been eating when she first wrote to me), and a pair of headphones. There was more evidence of her in my apartment than of me, or anything that came before. It had been three weeks.

In our first conversation, Amaia told me how that morning

her whole family had watched her oldest brother, a heroin addict, get arrested outside of their church. She said this the way that I told people my biological father was a drug addict who, last I heard, lived in a trailer in Florida. The way I told people that I used to be a heroin addict, a dominatrix.

Tell me about the room you're in, I asked her. *What's on the walls?* She described a painting of a woman in bondage. A set of silver longhorns, their gleaming tapered points.

What's on your walls? she asked me.

Nothing, I said.

We wrote long e-mails every night, and at first the lyrical nature of her letters struck me. *Really?* I thought. They were all image and intensity. Lines broken like those of a poem. Weighted, as if she were already imagining our correspondence in retrospect. As if she were building the myth of us. It was an alluring perspective; in it, I was a tragic beauty, herself a doomed hero. It was the kind of story that I'd loved as a girl, when everything seemed tragic and romantic, the kind of story that only ended in a wedding or a funeral.

I wasn't surprised to find that her favorite books were the *Iliad* and the *Odyssey*. Like Homer's stories, ours began *in medias res*. It was full of passion and conflict and tears of all kinds. Like Achilles returns Chryseis to her father, she would eventually return me to mine, and also for a price. In Greek dramas, every gift comes at a price. Like Odysseus, she crossed the country for me. But Odysseus's name means *trouble* in Greek, and his heroic gift is *metis* (μῆτις)—cunning intelligence, not *good communication* or *physical and emotional availability*. Odysseus is a deceptive wordsmith. He is prone to disguise. He is proud and passionate, but not loyal. Amaia was not Odysseus, but she loved such heroes, and her sense of narrative was epic.

After that first conversation, we spoke on the phone almost every day, though never at night. Her wife was an elementary school teacher and home by midafternoon. I didn't ask about the wife. I told her what I loved: the city, my family, powdered coffee creamer, the cigarettes I'd recently begun smoking again. No one in my family loved cigarettes or powdered creamer—among them, I had always been an outlier in my tastes.

Powdered creamer? Amaia laughed. *You are such an Indian.*

My ears tingled. *You are* is a powerful thing to say to a person. All my life I had insisted: *I am, I am, I am.* But privately, I never stopped looking. Compulsive bibliomancer, I opened to random pages in books, ran my blind finger down the page—looking for words to live by. I read the dictionary looking for a definition that fit. I took personality tests in magazines. I read horoscopes. I scoured the *DSM–IV*. I scrutinized the gaze of others, of mirrors, of lovers.

I told her about my days and the things that filled them. I told her about my friends.

I can't keep track, she said. I paused when the subway rushed by, a wave crashing over us. *You are a blur*, she said. *You are a train. You never stop moving. I wonder if I could stop you.*

Stop me, I thought.

6

My first diary was full of lists. Behind its wintergreen cover and exquisitely miniature lock, on its gold-leafed pages I maintained comprehensive records of the books I read. How else would I know when I had finished them all, as I intended? I listed the books I wanted to read, art I wanted to see, albums to acquire, films to watch. I kept meticulous lists of songs I loved, places I wanted to travel, projected earnings from summer jobs, my friends in descending order of endearment, and later, with an elaborate code signifying the degree of my physical accomplishment—the people I wanted to seduce.

It was an early form of self-soothing. I listed myself to

sleep. I ticked off items on my fingers on the school bus. As a teen, I made mixtape after mixtape, agonizing over order and annotating their playlists in the finest tipped pens.

In March of 2014, I saw Lorraine Hansberry's notebooks in an exhibit at the Brooklyn Museum. The writer of *A Raisin in the Sun*, Hansberry was also a lister. Every year between her late twenties and early thirties, she repeated inventories with the headings: *I like, I hate, I want, I am bored with.* At twenty-eight, the year before *A Raisin in the Sun* debuted, she likes *Renee Kaplan's legs, slacks, being hungry, conversations with James Baldwin,* and *Eartha Kitt's eyes, voice, legs, & music.*

She hates *loneliness, pictures of myself,* and *people who don't appreciate Kitt*; is bored by *A Raisin in the Sun,* and *most sexual experiences.* She wants *to be in love.*

At thirty-one, she loves *the sweet innocence of certain raucous lesbians I know, hazel eyes apparently, the first drink of scotch, the second,* and *the third.*

At thirty-two, she loves *69 when it really works, the inside of a lovely woman's mouth, some ideas of Brecht's,* and *those rare mornings when I wake without unhappiness.*

At thirty-two, she hates *my fears, my god-awful fears of almost everything,* and introduces the new category: *I regret.*

Read sequentially, they make a bildungsroman of lists—a story of sexual awakening in which maturity is signified by the discovery of regret. My story did not include regret until thirty-two, either, the age at which, like Hansberry, I came to truly know my own fear.

I spent a long time at the museum that day, hunched over the glass boxes that held her notebooks. Her lists helped me understand my own impulse to inventory. Hansberry was studying herself, tracking her own patterns, interrogating her tastes—trying to know herself. She was chasing down her hidden parts, arranging their clues in comforting rows, lining up the evidence like bruised cans on a pantry shelf, or suspects in a lineup.

Hansberry was always a political writer—an outspoken Civil Rights activist, she was friend to James Baldwin and Nina Simone (who wrote the song "To Be Young, Gifted and Black" in memory of her)—but she was never a lesbian writer. At that time, there hardly was such a thing. Maybe being a black writer was marginal enough. She wasn't even sure that she *was* a lesbian, until later in her career.

The unseen parts of us have the most gravity. They repel and compel us. My entire life, I've dreamt of chasing and being chased. I've felt like a specter haunting my own life, though I know that objectively I appear substantial and defined.

The urge to list is an urge to locate and to contain. A list is an attempt to organize the chaos both inside and outside of us into something manageable, finite. It is the same urge that drives diagnoses, blood quantum, gender definition, IQ tests, rubrics, personality types, and self-quizzes. I've read the word "compulsion" defined as an action repeated to relieve a mental obsession. A list, like a drink, is a symptom. It is the scratch at an itch on the scalp of a whirring brain. It is a worrying, and like a worry, it is a sign of some deeper concern.

7

A month after our first kiss, she bought me a ticket to Santa Fe. I flew to her a few days after my thirty-second birthday. On that plane, I shook. I had dismantled my life, and was flying across the country to meet a stranger. What would I feel when I saw her? Would I feel nothing? Would I turn around and get back on a plane? Would I suffer through the incredible awkwardness of that misplaced bet?

The color scheme of Albuquerque "Sunport" is desert: turquoise, pink, sand beige. Walking through it, I felt weight-less as a sun-bleached bone, a thing lost to the structure that defines it.

I saw her first, slouched in cutoff jeans and T-shirt, body a curved S, hair hung over her shoulders as she stared at her phone. I saw in her the vulnerability of not knowing she was being watched. She looked up and her smile was nervous and real, and in it I saw what she'd looked like as a child. In the parking lot she set down my suitcase and took my face into her hands, her soft mouth landing me back into being.

We kissed on the hot leather seats of her rental car, mouths tentative at first, hands drifting up to each others' faces, then hungrier. On the drive back to the hotel I was so wet that I feared it would show through my dress so I leaned on one hip in the passenger seat.

So much of our story is corporeal. I knew about somatic response, how the body takes what the psyche cannot bear and understands it as fever, as sweat and cramp, as cry, as come. But those were concepts. I had never lost my mind in this way, abandoned understanding to the body.

Sex had always featured large in my life. By this I mean the things that surround sex. It had loomed in my own self-conception, and so in others' perception of me. My body developed early, and I garnered a reputation as a slut in middle school, and was tormented daily for a short but form-ative time.

ABANDON ME

Despite, or because of this, I became obsessed with being wanted. Sexual desire was the easiest to elicit—a strange power that I could exercise but not control. In college, I became a sex worker. Years later, I wrote a book about having been a sex worker. But none of these things were sex. Nor did they ever seem connected to my actual experiences of sex. I had done things for money that would shock most people, but of actual intimacy and pleasure, I had a small catalog. I had loved a few times and never made love with the lights on.

I was so young when I started acting the part. After I quit the dungeon and the drugs, I came back to a self who had been buried under those masks. I discovered that I did not enjoy sex with lovers whom I did not love. Or was not at least beginning to love. And even then I never forgot myself. I discovered at nearly thirty years old that I was shy.

In the hotel room, Amaia undressed me. I knelt on the bed, and she paused to look at me. It was late afternoon and still daylight. We did not draw the shades. I had never felt so naked, but her gaze was shadow-soft. Then she undressed, and I forgot myself. Her lean length, so different from my own shape, so similar in ways I'd never touched: her smooth skin and dark nipples, her long hair.

The first time she asked me to come, she asked in Spanish, the Captain's first language. It felt like a consummation. Not of love, per se, but a desire stored deep in our bodies. *This*, we said with our hands and teeth and tongues. *This is as close as we can get to it. This is everything, and it is not enough.* I understood what she had meant when she wrote that I had taken something from her. I wanted something from her that I could not name. My whole body was a mouth. My heart was a mouth that only she could fill, that she could never fill.

The next morning I woke to her hands on me. Later she told me that she did not sleep at all. Her hands on my belly, my breasts, clasping my shoulder blades, my hips, my neck—it felt like she was building me. To be rebuilt, we must first be demolished. And by the end of that first month, I was already undone.

8

Though I was born in a tiny town near the Massachusetts border of Connecticut—I grew up mostly on Cape Cod, just a few miles from the largest Wampanoag population in this country. The summer we moved next to the Mashpee tribe, the Captain took me to their yearly Powwow. I was nine years old and had voyaged on the Captain's ship. I had seen the bazaars of Tangier and smelled the dank tombs of the Giza pyramids. I had walked through the Valley of the Kings in Luxor. But I had never seen an Indian.

Like much of coastal Massachusetts, Cape Cod has a large Cape Verdean population. From the early nineteenth century, whaling ships—whose crews included many Wampanoag—would pick up seamen from the small Portuguese fishing island on their regular routes. Like the Wampanoag, they were hard workers, and hired for little pay. By the early twentieth century, Cape Verdeans flooded the whaling capitals of New England, where they could earn money to send home to their drought-stricken island.

With my olive skin, green eyes, and straight hair, I resembled the descendants of these whalers, who had mixed with European settlers and African slaves.

Are you Portuguese? my classmates would ask, as early as elementary school.

No, I'd answer. *I'm Indian.* I didn't know what that meant. Only that I had parts that hadn't come from my parents. Parts linked to a different history, to people outside of my family, to whom no one else was connected.

It meant that I did not belong to their group—whose members all had similar names, names I've since seen on early crew lists in whaling museums: Gonsalves, Lopes,

Cardoza, Texiera, Mendes. The Cape Verdeans had a club-house in town, and cousins by the handful. Though my name also came from a small island of seafaring brown people—Puerto Rico—no one recognized it. My cousins were blonde girls in the New Jersey suburbs. And though I knew the Wampanoag lived just one town over, a five-minute drive from our home, I had never met one.

On a field trip to Plymouth Rock, when my teachers asked my classmates to imagine the sweet sight of land after months at sea, I imagined the sight of the *Mayflower* gliding out from the horizon, a white-winged colossus crashing into the shore, spilling bleached bodies. I wondered if anyone recognized their undoing in those hungry faces. I knew they hadn't. But I wished that they had cut down those pilgrims as their feet touched the ground, felled them like pale stalks of corn.

9

The day after I returned to New York, we were on the phone. I had just stepped out of the shower and stood nude in my room. I was still drunk on our sex, languid and distracted, never not thinking of her. I pulled on my underwear.

My wife knows, she told me. I didn't ask how or how

much. Maybe they were already sleeping in separate rooms. No one was talking about leaving.

What do you think? she asked me.

I answered without hesitation. It seemed obvious. *I'm fine with this*, I told her, and I was. *But I probably won't be after a while.* I wasn't interested in being anyone's mistress. Who is? *I guess we just do what feels right until it doesn't feel right anymore, don't you think?*

She got quiet and then we hung up. I didn't think much of it. I didn't think it had been a test. I didn't realize I'd set a limit.

An hour later, standing outside of a meeting in Manhattan, I got her e-mail. She was thinking of me, she said. *Your unstoppable hips. The motion of them. And your mouth. I've been on my knees for your mouth since I first found it.* But she had also been thinking about our *strange talk*. What talk? Had it been strange? I wondered. *Something feels wrong*, she said. *And I know you are doing what you want until you don't want to do it anymore. Maybe that is it.* She was ending it. *I will leave you alone now*, she said, as if I'd asked for such a thing.

It was the first time anyone had ever broken up with me. It was a thing I had successfully avoided for thirty-two years. We weren't even a couple yet. I stood outside that meeting, reading her e-mail, and I felt myself break. I called her but she didn't answer. I called and called. I walked into the meeting and sat for an hour. Heard nothing but the sound of breaking.

I walked home across the Manhattan Bridge. I was not myself. I was no longer a woman. I was the sound of breaking. Pedestrians and bicyclists looked around, covered their ears. My new roommate did not see or hear me unlock the door of the apartment. He went to his room. I sat in the kitchen, shivering. What had I said? It was the first time I thought, *I will do anything.* Her withdrawal opened a chasm in me, and I would do anything to fill it.

When she finally answered the phone, I said, *Listen. I am breaking. I will do anything.*

What do you want? she asked me.

I want you, I said, and could hear that she was glad.

Sometimes, she said, *"want" and "need" are the same thing.*

10

The powwow grounds smelled of hay and smoke and fry bread and bodies. Indian bodies. All around us. Just minutes out of the car, I saw that *Indian* meant a thousand things that I'd never known. Sellers hawked blankets from tables in labyrinthine rows around the perimeter of the field. They sold baskets and pottery and belts and jewelry on deerskin strips beaded with wampum carved from quahogs and conch shells. A tall muscled man in fringed leather and headband carved a canoe from a felled tree.

In the middle of that field, they danced all day. They circle danced, blanket danced, grass danced, and fancy danced. I watched their feet stomp and tear up the grass until the ground was bald dirt, dust clouds, the women's skirts darkened at the hems. Their drums shook my chest. I had a stomping in me. Something to give of my body, to my body, to beat into the ground. I felt it there, and it felt more solid than anything else in me.

But when the Captain got to talking with an Elder—a woman whom he still says he was drawn to because her face looked like what my face might look at her age—and she offered to teach me those dances, said that I could join them, that there was enough blood in me to belong there, I shook my head. I clung to the Captain's arm, and said no.

I was nine and already felt, *I am not enough of this. For this.* I already believed that some things were given and not sought. I understand now that he was trying to give me something. But it was too late. I was already finding other ways to anchor myself in this world.

After dark, the Wampanoag men played a game called Fireball. Like soccer, it consists of two goals, and a ball to kick through them. Unlike soccer, the players are permitted to use their hands. And the ball—constructed of wire mesh and a bundle of kerosene-soaked rags—is on fire. It is a medicine game. Before it begins, all the men think of suffering loved ones, living and passed, and pray that the pain they feel when the fireball scorches their hands and feet lessens the suffering of others.

In the dark, we stood amid the crowd. We watched that flaming ball soar across the field. We smelled its burning. We could not see the players, only the flickering of that blaze as their bodies passed between us and it—less men than un-fire, than darkness gathered into form, into muscle and grunt. When the ball neared the goals, the crowd roared, their bodies leaning in. *Pick it up*, they screamed, *Pick it up!*

I didn't need to belong to feel that fire, to understand that a burning thing could heal, if you were willing to take it in your hands.

11

For the first year, I could not go to her home. She came to New York, and we met in other places. In November, she gave a lecture at a large university in Ohio. We met in the airport and the young woman who had booked her drove us to our hotel. I sat in the backseat of the young woman's car and Amaia in the passenger seat. As the two of them spoke, their tones more familiar than I had expected, I watched Amaia tap her hand against the young woman's thigh for emphasis. I watched the young woman look at Amaia.

How do you know her? I asked later at the hotel.

From online, she shrugged. *Just e-mailing.*

That weekend, Hurricane Sandy trapped us in Ohio, watching New York get pummeled from the hotel television. The rooms of the boutique hotel were themed, and ours was the Treehouse. A canopy of smooth branches crowned our bed, and orange lights glowed on the bedside tables. We were only a few states away from New York, but it might have been another world.

Fantastical worlds had always seduced me. I had built such worlds in love. And the stories I loved most were of this kind.

My favorite film at fourteen was Peter Jackson's *Heavenly Creatures*. The story tells of two New Zealand teens—Juliet and Pauline—who meet in school and fall into a rapturous kind of love. Juliet is played by a young Kate Winslet. She is beautiful and charismatic. She reframes their ordinary lives with masterful invention. And in her conception, they swell with romance and drama. Juliet transforms Pauline into a tragic and noble heroine, and Pauline forms, in the words of her doctor, an "unhealthy attachment" to Juliet. The two girls begin writing a novel together about a world that Juliet names Borovnia. In Borovnia, the dramas of their daily lives are translated into mythological proportions. The Borovnian scenes depicted in the film are lush and magical. They are vibrant as Oz in Technicolor. The boundaries between their real lives and their fantasies blur, and ultimately the magic ends in murder. It is a visually magnificent film, and as profound and accurate a depiction of fantasy's power as any I have seen or read. At fourteen, I had had such rapturous affairs with other girls, had departed into the worlds of them, and though none were so undifferentiated from reality, I recognized the truth in Jackson's film, about the power of illusion and of story—how believing in it could save you, could steal you, and become the real.

Where did you come from? Amaia asked me, cupping my face in her hands, voice breathy with wonder. She splayed her fingers across my chest, belly, and hips—measured every part of me with her palms. I was a marvel. I was her Pandora. And her desires were the gods who created me. *You are so beautiful*, she said again and again. *Your mouth, your mouth reinvents the word "mouth."*

I squirmed under this scrutiny, laughed, but she stayed serious.

Your hips, she said, pressing her mouth against them. *I didn't know what hips were before yours.*

Yeah, right, I murmured, burying my fingers in her hair.

I mean it, she said. *Touching you makes me feel like I have a hundred hands, makes me wish I had a hundred more.*

Hesiod doesn't name Pandora in his *Theogony*; she is only a "beautiful evil," the sight of whom seizes gods and mortals alike with wonder.

My girl, Amaia murmured, and repeated my name like a mantra, until it felt like a word carved by her mouth. Until I couldn't remember what it had meant before she spoke it.

Our last day, we made love all afternoon, and at midnight she walked a mile to bring me back a piece of chocolate cake, tarry with sugared frosting. We ate the cake, and made love again, our mouths sweet, her hair smelling of the winter outside.

Then she went quiet. Now I knew better. Worry sawed in my gut.

What's wrong? I asked her.

Nothing, she said. I scoured the afternoon, searched for something I'd missed. I began to cry.

I tried many ways to name that feeling. For her and later for myself. The most accurate description and the one I give here is not mine. It is from *The NeverEnding Story*. The film's protagonist is a native boy—Atreyu, an orphan. The antagonist is a force called the Nothing. The Nothing consumes all in its path, annihilates all life with its infectious despair. Even its name is a riddle, a vacuum—it can't be fought. Like Odysseus, who tells the Cyclops Polyphemus that his name is Nobody. When Odysseus blinds the Cyclops, the Cyclops cries out that "Nobody" has blinded him, and no one understands or believes in his pain.

The feeling Amaia's silence triggered in me was a Nothing, a Nobody. I could not name it—like hunger, it was an emptiness, an emptier.

We sat in that hotel room under the bed's dark branches. She in her silence and me in my Nothing.

Finally, she explained. *Te amo*, she said. *I need you.*

The next morning, the storm had grounded all planes. She left the hotel room to call home and say that she was delayed. We rented a car and drove through the next night, eleven hours down ghosted highways strewn with tree limbs. Near dawn, when we emerged from the Lincoln Tunnel, the city itself had been ravaged by a Nothing. The streetlamps, stoplights; all that neon snuffed out. Awnings torn from storefronts. Abandoned.

I glided across this new Manhattan, eyes burning with exhaustion. The world had lost its pulse, but with her beside me, it no longer mattered. That morning, I understood that to love me terrified her, the way losing her terrified me. I knew that she had suffered losses as a child and that she was slow to trust. I will take care of her, I thought. I will show her it is safe to love me. I will empty the streets of my life for her. I will become a city for her alone.

12

As a little girl, I could eat as much as a man. The Bottomless Pit, my mother called me. We did not have the same snacks in our cupboard as my friends did. But I still ate our nuts and dried fruits until they were gone, until my stomach bloated, until my mother waved the empty jars at me. *You're not even hungry!* she'd say. *You can't be.* But I was hungry. For food, for approval, for secrets, for my legs' push against the ground, for the ocean, for words. For none of these things at all, but for the brief satisfaction of filling myself with them.

My hunger was a dark spot behind my solar plexus, its gravity so great that I felt the tug in my fingers and toes. I pressed my hands under my ribs. I filled a bag with food from our kitchen and took it to my room. In my room I read and I ate. I didn't feel hungry. I didn't feel anything. I didn't even exist. It was perfect. Then, one afternoon, I went into the tiny half-bath and dug my hand down my throat. Even then I had big hands. I reached into my body and emptied it. After, I lay in my bed and kept reading. It was a different kind of full, this emptiness.

I was eleven. My body had begun turning against me, swelling outward. It was the summer before I learned that its burning could be a power that eased other hurts, other hungers. For a while, it would be the only medicine I needed. But the summer I was eleven, I was going to baseball camp.

The morning that camp began, my parents sat me down in the kitchen. They knew. The Captain had heard me and found a mess in the bathroom. They didn't know what to do. They wanted me to explain. How could I? Would I have said that I was hungry? That the emptiness filled me? That the sickness was a cure? That I was burning up? I was eleven. I had been fine my whole life. I had never asked for help. I was helping myself.

Why? he asked. He looked at me in confusion, and something like disgust. I don't think that I disgusted him. I think he didn't recognize me, saw something in me that scared him. I think he meant, *Who are you?*

I had no answers. I didn't want to go to baseball camp, but they insisted. He silently drove me to a green sprawl of fields from which I could see the ocean. I got out of the car and stood in that field. I covered my face with my glove and tasted the palm of its leather hand. I trailed behind the herd of boys as they corralled us from one station to the next. I scooped up grounders and caught flies. I watched those waves roll endlessly in, smashing on the shore.

When I got to the pitching machine, I lifted my elbow and squinted and swung. Ball after ball, I aimed for that shore, for the ocean beyond. Each ball was a piñata of my body. Seven points for seven sins and a belly full of temptation. I smashed it to pieces, all that sweetness raining down over us like confetti. The boys cheered. They called me Mrs. Babe Ruth. The Home Run Queen.

13

The Texas airport was the smallest we'd met in—a single baggage carousel, where I waited for her in a pair of bright green pants. I was nervous, afraid that when I saw her, I would feel nothing. It had become a familiar fear, one that

I felt in every airport. I called a close friend—Amit—an Israeli writer whom I trusted to always tell me the truth.

What if I feel nothing this time? I said. *You won't*, she assured me. She was the only friend I talked to about my new love, and I asked her the same questions over and over—what if she leaves? What if I can't take this? *She won't*, Amit said. *You can.*

In the rental car we kissed and kissed. She put her hands on me and my hips went rocking. She laughed, *There go those hips!*

I can't help it, I said. *They are like those windup teeth, they just go, chattering across the floor.* She laughed again. *Exactly.* She loved her effect on me. It was romantic, or easy to see that way. I had loved before, but I had never known this mechanical insistence of my own body. It was a physical reaction absent of sense or control, its inertia unbound by consciousness. The dog that will eat until its stomach splits. The car that will drive itself off a cliff. The anorectic. The addict.

Halfway to our remote destination, we pulled over on the side of the road and made love. The sky was bigger than any I'd seen, and the setting sun had streaked it pink—bright veins of lit neon, splayed over the desert, my leg on the dashboard. As she opened her mouth on me, the sky blurred. She didn't ask me why I was crying, but pressed her hands against my face, my hair, my shaking shoulders. *I am in love*, I told myself.

No lover had ever left me. I had spent enough years in therapy to know this was not something to brag about. I was far from perfect. I worked hard at my relationships. I loved a lot, but always a little less than my lovers. In the beginnings, I always knew that if someone left, it would be me. It always was. I worried the riddle: if I never love anyone who can hurt me, they never will. But what if I can never love those people enough to stay?

The Imago Theory of relationships posits that we are born whole and complete, but are wounded during early stages of development by our primary caretakers. Deep in our unconscious mind, we form a composite image of all the positive and negative traits of those caretakers. This is the Imago. It is the blueprint of what we are looking for in love. It is the person who is capable of healing us, and of hurting us the most. We will reenact our childhood narratives until, if ever, we get a better ending.

I understood this theory before I ever read about it. I understood that nearly every article about "choosing" a lover, about cataloging the qualities you look for in a spouse, was full of shit. We are never looking for someone with a good sense of humor or who likes children. No one is "good" in bed. At least, these are not the things that make us love them. Falling in love is always the fear and promise of being hurt, of being healed.

According to Freud, *cathexis* (translated from the German *besetzung,* by James Strachey) is the investment of psycho-sexual energy in an object or person. It is the teddy bear. It is the wedding ring. It is art. It is story. It is every symbol. It is the projection on the lover that we call falling in love. Freud posed cathexis and de-cathexis as natural and necessary parts of development. But when the ego, or some other force, interrupts or blocks the process, a person can form alternate dynamics—addiction, reaction forma-tion, neuroticism.

M. Scott Peck, in his 1970s bestseller, *The Road Less Traveled*—a prominent spine on my mother's bookshelf—defines love as "The will to extend one's self for the purpose of nurturing one's own or another's spiritual growth." Our fantasy of love is mere cathexis, he asserted. Love is not a feeling, a fever, or need; "Love is as love does."

Every pop song on the radio is an anthem to an Imago—the compulsive, consuming, devastating, regressive, mad attachment that goes all the way back to the beginning of us, to our oldest need, when love really was the thing that kept us alive. Most of these songs are more aptly addressed from a child to a parent or a parent to a child: "Sweet Child o' Mine," "Wrecking Ball," "Bleeding Love," "I Can't Live Without Your Love," "When Something Is Wrong with My Baby," and on and on. Abandonment by a lover won't kill us. But it awakens the parts of us that remember when it could.

14

My mother took me to meet Jon once. In eight years, he had never called, never written or sent a birthday card.

His life then existed in a trailer beside his parents' trailer in Florida, which felt, in summer, like the inside of a fevered mouth. His mother, my grandmother, was a year from dying. A large woman, she sat in a chair in her trailer, lap draped in an orange afghan, smoking. Everything in the trailer was yellowed with smoke, even her face and hands. She coughed—part rattle, part roar from the sticky depths of her big body—as if something were being dragged, or fighting its way out, as if a crow might flap from her mouth. Her gaze never wandered. She offered me chips and candy, things my mother didn't keep in our home, and she watched me eat them.

I almost forgot he was there. A man dark as the Captain, but smaller, blurry around the edges. When they suggested he play me a song, he led me up the metal stairs into his trailer. *Here*, he said, and handed me a stuffed monkey. He played a song, and I waited for him to finish. I thought, *I should not be in this trailer with this stranger, with this strange man.* When he smiled, I wanted to leave worst of all.

Before my mother brought us back north, we saw an alligator. I remember the alligator better than I remember Jon. The way it lay there in the swampy shallows. The blinking eyes. If a small crowd hadn't gathered to point, it would have gone unseen. With its algae-slick scales, it was exactly what should crawl out of those waters. With no fence between us, no double-thick glass terrarium walls, I thrilled at the proximity. It was only a degree of hunger between those teeth and me.

15

I brought Carl Jung's *Red Book* to Texas in my suitcase. The size of a serving tray, it weighed at least fifteen pounds and I joked with my therapist mother about my *heavy psychological baggage.* My own therapist was a Jungian and would sometimes offer quotes of his. They always struck me as true, so I'd started reading him, which I hadn't done since college.

In 1913, after he and Freud had a falling out, Jung exiled himself for seven years. He dug into his own psyche in what he called a "confrontation with the unconscious," and faced everything: his demons, his gods, his wounds, and his desires. During this time, he recorded his findings, translated his emotions into images. It took him sixteen years afterward to create the *Liber Novus, the Red Book*—205 pages of calligraphic text and full-color illustrations. All of the images were drawn by Jung's own hand. At first look I felt that he'd drawn them for me. There is the Hekatonkheir, the Centimani with his hundred hands reaching, bent over backward with a snake's tail. There are ouroboroi and spiraled mandalas and moon-glowed trees. There is a monster hidden beneath a boat at sea. *The Red Book* is the basis of all Jung's future work—his theories of archetypes, the collective unconscious, and active imagination. In *Memories, Dreams, Reflections* he says: "That was the stuff and material for more than only one life. Everything later was merely the outer classification, scientific elaboration, and the integration into life. But the numinous beginning, which contained everything, was then."

As Amaia and I wandered around that dusty little town, stopping often to eat and chat with strangers, I thought about Jung. I thought about going back to the beginning. Most people dismissed Jung at the time. They thought he had lost his mind. That he had just suffered a seven-year nervous breakdown. A nervous breakdown is a coup of the psyche—forces that refuse to be repressed any longer. I have found it true: that what the mind refuses, the body will eventually take. But Jung was not a victim of his own repressed psyche. He made a choice to yield to it. He knew that exiling oneself to the desert of one's own mind was a necessary kind of madness. It precluded nervous breakdown. Jung wanted to teach people about the Self, and he knew that he had to face the darkest parts of his own if he wanted to show anyone it could be done.

I was no Carl Jung. I was a thirty-two-year-old writer in a long distance relationship. Who spent too much time on Facebook. But I also knew that having gone to the darkest places in myself and come back, that having written that story, was the most useful thing I'd ever done. I wasn't going to disappear for seven years. But I was gathering courage. I was preparing to face something that I knew was going to hurt.

16

I dropped out of high school after freshman year to be my own teacher. The first thing I assigned myself was Howard

Zinn's *A People's History of the United States*. I read
Bartolome de las Casas's accounts of Columbus's colonization of the Arawaks and the Captain's Taino ancestors. I read
of Spaniards drunk on power, riding the backs of natives like
horses, slicing off pieces of their bodies to test the sharpness
of blades, and beheading native children for sport.

My mother had told me that I descended from the King
Philip tribe of the Wampanoag. The man the English settlers
called King Philip was Metacomet, and he led the
Wampanoag in 1675, when King Philip's War began. His
father, Massasoit, was the Wampanoag leader who helped
the pilgrims to survive. I never read his name in any text-
book, but there is a community college near Brockton,
Massachusetts, called Massasoit.

His son, Metacomet, grew up watching his people deci-
mated by disease and suffer the betrayals and brutalities of
the colonists. After years of trying to sustain good relations,
he led a revolt that ended on August 12, 1676, when
he was drawn and quartered, ending a bloody two-year
war. His decapitated head was displayed in Plymouth for
twenty years. The few remaining Wampanoag, including
Metacomet's wife and children, were enslaved and sold in
Bermuda, or placed in other tribes as captives and tribal
members. The Wampanoag tribe, as well as the Narragansett,
Podunk, Nipmuck, and others, was virtually eliminated.

There were bumper stickers in our liberal town that read NO WAR. Even as a child, I was struck by the naïveté of such a sentiment. Who wanted war? War was what happened. War had won us our easy lives. Bumper stickers were a spoil of war. The luxury of denouncing war was a spoil of wars won. But this was different. This was a genocide that had been erased—not a secret, but a choice. What, I wondered, if the Nazis had won? I would have learned their glory in my history books. I might never have met a Jew, as I had never met an Indian, though they were the namesakes of the streets in my town, the beaches where I swam, the villages that surrounded us. I lay in my room and cried.

I knew that I wasn't any Indian princess. I wasn't even an Indian. But Indian was something that had been given to me from the beginning. Just a word, a container for me to fill, or to fill with me. I knew that that history was part mine. That there was nothing to trust in this world.

17

In 2010, two weeks before my first book was published, Jon sent me a friend request on Facebook.

Are you yourself? I asked.

Yes I am, he said. *Man this is amazing I'm so excited.*

A few hours later another message.

Hi monkey, it said.

Monkey was also a nickname that my then-girlfriend called me.

Did you. Know I have a monkey tatoo.

Two days later he wrote me again.

Hi milissa.

He offered to have his sister, Joan, send me a CD of his original songs.

I gave him the address of my post office box but never received anything.

At first, I didn't tell anyone about our interaction. I felt embarrassed for both of us. What kind of man behaves like this? I didn't know how I felt, or if I felt anything. I feared that if someone pitied me then I'd start pitying myself. I had always framed my story as a triumph, a lucky turn to have found my true father at two years old. The book I was about to publish was similar—a dark story, a story of self-destruction that had led to transformation. This was my life. First dark, then light. But the dark was my first instinct, and perhaps my truest. My worst fear was that it would always find me, that eventually, it would win. I had been lucky. But if I felt it—*really* felt it, if I let it in, if I let *him* in, I might never find my way out of it again.

Kissinger wrote that "History is the memory of states." If that memory were recorded in my history textbooks and on the plaques of historical monuments, then where, I wondered, were the memories of the dead recorded? Where was the history of the people who survived them?

The French philosopher Theodule Ribot, in his 1881 work, *The Maladies of Memory*, claimed memory's location in the nervous system, and thusly of material nature. Henri Bergson, in his rebuttal to Ribot—*Matter and Memory*—made a distinction between practical memory and pure memory, the latter of which trades in "image remembrance." Bergson believed that the more a spirit draws from this true memory, and exists in an awareness of the past in conjunction with the immediacy of bodily experience, the more conscious she becomes. Impulsivity, according to the philosopher, is the symptom of a person trapped in her corporeal present, accessing only her practical memory. Despite their contention, both philosophers support what I knew empirically by fifteen—to exist in my body, and to hold the memory of my history, was to be searingly awake. I was not awake. I had exiled large swathes of my history, and been denied others. I had spent long stretches of time divorced from my body. I was a piñata, rattling with impulse and temptation, reacting to forces whose origins were mysterious to me.

My therapist once said, *When we don't react, something creative happens.* She meant that we get to fully experience what happens. When we observe how the world affects us and let our defenses rest, when we consider the context of our greater history, we have an opportunity to act from our higher selves and perceptions. Not reacting gives us the agency to change. Or, in the famous words of Spanish philosopher George Santayana, *Those who cannot remember the past are doomed to repeat it.* To repeat their same reactions to it for all time, despite even self-annihilation. It was a truth I beat my head against even as a child. Why did self-knowledge not stop me from repeating the same painful acts? Why this insanity as Einstein defined it—the repetition of the same act with an expectation of a different result? The bondage of reaction is stronger even than that of self-preservation.

Santayana also said that *history is nothing but recorded and assisted memory.* And that *when experience is not retained, as among savages, infancy is perpetual.* I don't think he had the addict in mind when he wrote this, but I know no clearer proof than of that savage state. I don't think he had the erased history of the Indigenous American or their perpetual subjugation by a reactive government in mind when he used the word *savage*, but it is appropriate in ways he did not intend.

In the small Texas town, the trains ran all day. Each morning, we woke at dawn and sat in an orange chair by the window to watch the sun rise, spill its mad colors across that enormous sky. Every sunrise was a carnival of color, to the soundtrack of those trains. They barreled across the desert and their rumble in my chest, the bleat of those whistles, reminded me of the foghorns on the Cape. *Whistle* is too weak a word. When a human makes such a sound, it expresses only a few things: terrible grief, earth-shattering climax, triumph, or pain. Not broken-finger pain, but dying pain, child-birthing pain. That kind of sound is all body, all heart, out of mind. It's ironic that both train whistles and fog horns should evoke such animal feeling, as they both exist specifically for their listeners. *Here I come*, they say. *Get off the tracks if you don't want my two-hundred tons of steel barreling into your chest. Steer your prow elsewhere if you don't want to wreck against my shore.* Not a threat, but a warning: *I can't stop myself, so it's up to you, stranger.*

We ate buttery grilled cheese sandwiches from food trucks. We ate chocolates with molten centers and cayenne freckles. I gorged with her, and it was the only time I ate. I began to associate the feeling of a full belly with her. I also began to associate laughter with her. For all our intensity, we laughed a lot.

In my twenties I lived with a man for three years who never laughed at my jokes, never picked up the thread and unraveled it with me, never reached the punchline that was more body than words, a giddy orgasm shuddering through us. How had I done it? It must have been an important lesson, to stay so long.

I can't remember a time before this kind of laughter. My brother and I cut our teeth at the dinner table. There is nothing like a sad mother to make a kid funny. I had often thought that every joke was still for her.

Amaia knew how to build a joke, how to twist words and couple them the way I did, the way that delighted me. *How did you get so funny?* she would ask me with that marveling gaze, as if I had been designed with her in mind.

One afternoon, from a nearby café table, a local told us a story about a train conductor who'd fallen in love and had his heart broken by a woman in town. Every time he passed through, he'd sound his train's whistle all the way, borrowing its wail for his own so that the whole town could feel his busted heart hum in their chests, rattle their teeth, shake their skulls. And after that, every time a train passed and I heard that cry, I wondered if it was a warning or a wailing or a hallelujah. I thought of my own heart, how much I feared her breaking it. It would sound like that, I thought. It would be the only sound I ever heard again. It would be wrecking against the shore of one person for the rest of my life.

I feared it so much that I broke my own heart every day that I loved her. I felt it when I watched her reading in a café, absentmindedly scratching her head and twirling a pen with her long fingers. I felt it when we drove thirty miles to swim in a pool of water risen from deep underground, her skin warm and smooth as clay under my hands. On the way back we stopped at the "Largest Rattlesnake Exhibit on the Planet," where we paid five dollars to two petrified men in a warehouse with a hand-painted sign, steeped in the rot-dirt stench of snake shit, and stood in front of a rattler yellow as a fingernail and thicker than her long leg leaned against me, and I whispered that I didn't have any underwear on because I had swam in them, and she laughed and told me a lady should always wear underpants to visit the Largest Rattlesnake Exhibit on the Planet; I felt it. When I made love to her in that chair by the window, dawn glowing her body like a fruit split open to its wet center, I felt it—the way you feel a fall just looking over the edge of a roof.

Will you love me forever? she asked me. *Yes,* I said.

I couldn't know, though. When that whistle spills over the desert, you can only hear the call of your own heart. When I looked at her, I wondered. Are you my wrecking shore? Are you my third rail? Or are you my hallelujah?

20

In 2009, I dreamt of King Philip's War, of the woods behind my childhood home, and of a language whose sounds still moved in my mouth when I woke up in my Brooklyn apartment. I started writing. I bought books. For a month I thought about little else. I kept it to myself.

Months after the dream, I had lunch with my literary agent. *This story*, I said, *is calling to me. I don't know how to stop listening.*

He was quiet. He stared at his salad. *Readers*, he told me, *aren't into Native Americans. Have you ever read a book about Native Americans?*

Yes, I said. Even he had heard of Sherman Alexie.

Eh, he said. *Dreams are boring. And historical fiction?* He shrugged. *You*, he said, *have just written a book about being a dominatrix. Why don't you write something more urban, more edgy? Why don't you write something more you.*

I tried. I ignored the call of that story. But it would not go quiet. It took me five more years to listen. To understand that it was my own story calling. That no other person can say what rises to the surface, when it's ready.

21

What does it mean to retain experience? Psychologists, philosophers, teachers, and anthropologists agree that retention comes vis-à-vis reception, acknowledgement, repetition, and application. Retention happens *in memoriam*.

The theory of historical trauma was developed as an effort to understand the contemporary plight of Native Americans. It posits, according to a 2014 article by Dr. Kathleen Brown-Rice, that present-day natives experience "historical loss symptoms (e.g. depression, substance dependence, diabetes, dysfunctional parenting, unemployment) as a result of the cross-generational transmission of trauma from historical losses (e.g. loss of population, land, and culture)." There is marked skepticism in the mental health profession as to the validity of such a theory.

To clarify: among native populations, the rates of sexual and physical abuse, addiction, chronic illness, mental illness, poverty, and suicide are sometimes more than three times that of the national average, and there is doubt about the causal relationship between this and the five hundred years of purposeful and systematic destruction of Native American people by Europeans.

Between 1492, when Columbus came to America, and the establishment of the United States, the population of Native Americans fell by 95 percent. Native children of four and five years old were removed from their homes by the U.S. government and placed in boarding schools. They were forbidden contact with their families and communities. They could not speak their language. They could not practice their spiritual and cultural customs. And they were subjected, in many cases, to extreme forms of abuse. Native peoples were prevented from engaging in mourning rituals and oral transmission of their culture, history, and language.

A 2014 study—"Intergenerational transmission of emotional trauma through amygdala-dependent mother-to-infant transfer of specific fear" shows that trauma and fear communicated hormonally from mother to child permanently alters the brain, and can be then transmitted across generations. Studies show that the incidence of suicide among adolescents corresponds to a disconnection from their cultural past, and suicide is the second leading cause of death for Native Americans from ten to thirty-four years of age (Centers for Disease Control and Prevention [CDC], 2007). Native Americans are reported to have the highest poverty level of any group—minority or majority—in the United States (Denny, Holtzman, Goins, & Croft, 2005) and the lowest life expectancy of any population in the United States (CDC, 2010). A 2009 study (Kendell–Tackett) shows how trauma produces the hormones epinephrine and cortisol, which dramatically affect the body's blood sugar among myriad other functions. Accordingly, study subjects with PTSD report a significantly larger number of current and lifetime medical conditions than those without, including anemia, arthritis, asthma, back pain, diabetes, eczema, kidney disease, lung disease, and ulcers (Schnurr & Green, 2004; Weisberg et al., 2003)—all afflictions that occur in native populations at often three times the national average.

It goes on and on and on.

According to Whitbeck's Historical Loss Scale and Historical Loss Associated Symptoms Scale, 49 percent of surveyed natives have daily and "disturbing thoughts" about historical losses of language and culture. But only 22 percent of respondents indicated that they experienced discomfort with white people. One has to wonder where, then, a reaction is directed, if not toward the source of trauma. Our selves are sometimes the only things over which we wield power. And our means of expressing it are sometimes chosen for us.

After my parents found out, I stopped throwing up, but I didn't stop being hungry. Despite its gravity, a bottomless pit is an empty space. Hunger can saw at a body, but itself has no corners; it is force without shape, muscle without matter.

All my adult life, whenever the subject of my adolescence has arisen, my parents' faces go dark. The Captain has long referred to my twelfth through fourteenth years as the years *You were possessed*. When he says, *You were possessed*, I hear *You were not my daughter*. True, I stopped being good. With hairspray and curling irons, I transformed my soft baby hair into a shield—the crackle of it sounded so sweet to me. I never said no. I let men of eighteen and twenty and thirty years old trace the shape of my body. I stole liquor bottles and hid them in my dresser. I lied easily. My mother once cornered me in the hallway of our home and asked me if I was drunk. *No*, I told her. It was half true—no matter how much I drank, a part of me never slackened. *You're lying*, she said. *You're lying to my face.* She didn't even look angry. *What's in you?* she asked me.

Odd, that those years are the only years they consider me possessed. In the ones that followed, I became a junkie, a criminal—I took a new name and under that name I did things my parents' daughter never would. At twelve years old, though, I was still theirs. There was little in the world that had more influence on me. My mother was a Buddhist—she knew that even Siddhartha's parents could not protect him from suffering, from the world's ails, from his own destiny. Still, like them, she tried. She discouraged television and sugar and Barbie Dolls. It didn't matter—the thing that possessed me didn't come from television, or any doll box—it was in me. And in those later years, I simply learned to hide it better.

23

Amaia read an interview I'd given in a magazine in which I'd made some flippant jokes about having been a dominatrix.

You don't have to talk about yourself that way, she said. *It's crass. You are more than that*, she said. You are, you are.

You are mine, she said. *I don't want people to see you that way.* I hadn't thought that people saw me that way, though I remembered the time when they had. It scared me that I might still appear that way; that she might see something in me that I did not.

Sometimes, as we ate at restaurants with other people, Amaia would tap my knee under the table. It meant that the man with whom I was making small talk was too glad to be small-talking with me. I ought to stop. It meant that my voice was too loud. I had made a joke she found crude. I was chewing with my mouth open. I had never felt so uncouth. Or rather, no one had ever shown me this version of myself. If a friend had described this kind of monitoring, I would have thought, *never*. But what if that version of me were a true one?

I would want you to tell me, Amaia said.

A few months in, my friends began to say, *Where are you?* They never saw me anymore. We talked less. When we did, I only talked about her.

I had been building muscles of self-examination my whole adult life. When I tried to apply them with Amaia, to us, she didn't respond. *It feels like you pull away whenever I ask for something*, I said once, so nervous to point out the obvious. *I just want to talk about when our situation might change.*

You're frustrated, she said. *You have anger in you for me. I can't imagine feeling that for you.* She went quiet. *I'm not what you need*, she said. *I don't make you happy. Why don't we talk tomorrow.*

No, I said. *You make me happy! Please don't hang up.*

You don't talk about yourself anymore, a friend once

pointed out. When she asked me how I felt, I speculated about Amaia's feelings. When she asked me what I was going to do, I speculated about what Amaia would do, why she had done this or that.

It's like a tic, said my friend. *You never stop mapping her.* A cognitive behavioral therapist she'd seen for a while had once suggested a tool for redirecting obsessive thoughts: keep a rubber band around your wrist and every time the thought pattern takes over, snap it. *You should try it*, she said. The next day, I found a rubber band and slid it around my wrist. I snapped it over and over. My wrist stayed red and smarting. By afternoon, I took off the rubber band. I couldn't think straight with all that snapping.

Still, my friends understood. I was in love. I was going through something. They listened while I scrutinized our conversations, her actions, the way she never called me when she promised to, the way she planned trips for us and canceled them. The way she showered me with gifts. Every time she went quiet and the Nothing swept through me, I called Amit. *You're okay*, Amit said. *Just tell her what you need.*

The time we did spend together was fraught. When my phone lit up, Amaia frowned. She didn't understand why my friends needed me and why I felt obliged to them. She didn't understand why being out of touch with them made me anxious. *It's weird*, she said. *Amit isn't your girlfriend. I am.* She said I needed to trust myself more. I shouldn't put so much credence in what my friends thought. Real friends would understand that I was busy. That she came first.

One weekend, Amaia was giving a lecture at a college in Iowa. *Come*, she said. *You can get some writing done. There are too many distractions in New York.* I had always been a very disciplined writer, but I had not been writing. Not writing spread a layer of anxiety all through me. *You're too busy*, Amaia said, though I was mostly busy with her.

It was the weekend of my mother's birthday. My family had also begun to say, *Where are you?* I was on airplanes. I was on the phone with Amaia. I was waiting for Amaia to call me. I was scrutinizing our conversations.

I want you there, Amaia said.

I can't go, I said, my heart beating fast. I was driving to teach a class. My hands were sweating, which had become normal.

She was quiet. *Okay*, she said. *I understand.*

My family misses me, I said, as I pulled over to fill up at a gas station. *I just have to show up for some things.* I heard myself pleading. I didn't tell her that when I spoke to my mother, with whom I'd always been so close, it felt like a glass wall stood between us. My mother knocked on the wall. *Are you okay?* she kept asking. *I'm fine*, I'd say. I didn't feel fine but my instinct was to hide this. *I'm going through something*, I kept saying, like it was a car wash, and in a few minutes I'd roll out the other side of it, gleaming. *Okay,* my mother said. My brother, whom I had always called regularly, had barely heard from me in months. When we did speak, he didn't ask me what was wrong, but he didn't have to. I suspect he knew that I would explain when I was able.

The problem with being known is that your people know when you are gone.

It's fine, said Amaia. *You don't have to explain.*

It wasn't fine. By then, I was a master meteorologist of her moods. I unscrewed the gas cap and put it on the roof of the car, selected Regular. *I'll see you in another week, when you come here*, I reminded her, my pulse accelerating.

Please stop, she said. *I understand. This is hurting you. You are neglecting things.*

No, I said, becoming frantic. *It's not that. It's not that at all.* The gas tank full, I got back in the car and drove off, the gas cap bouncing in the road behind me. I was becoming careless. I *was* neglecting things. It was hard to think about Amaia and anything else at the same time. I had always been a pathologically punctual person, but a few days earlier, I had stood up a friend, completely forgotten our dinner plans.

I have to go, Amaia said, her voice distant.

Wait! I said, but she was gone.

It's all right, Amit said. *She's disappointed. Let her be disappointed. Let's get dinner or something.* Amit made it sound so easy, and I remembered thinking it could be easy, or at least tolerable, to disappoint someone. Now, I could not tolerate it. The night she flew to Iowa, I barely slept. I clutched the phone in my hand, and waited for some sign that she still loved me. I knew I should go to my mother's birthday party. I *wanted* to go to my mother's birthday party. But now I needed her permission, and it never came.

I bought a ticket to Iowa for the next morning. My mother was disappointed when I told her I wouldn't make it, but she understood. I didn't want to tell Amit, so I texted her from the airport. *Are you sure?* she wrote back. I didn't answer. What could I have said? It didn't feel like a choice.

I'm coming! I told Amaia.

My girl, she said. *You are coming.*

I love you, I said.

Now, why did you have to make that so hard? she said.

24

The Captain descends from *jíbaros*, indigenous Puerto Rican peasants who worked the colonial plantations. Like the Wampanoag, their ancestors were "discovered," infected, enslaved by *repartimiento*, executed, and exiled. Yes, Columbus tested his blades on both of my fathers' people. And alcohol eased those wounds, while making others. The Captain's father, my abuelo, had almost been murdered by my bisabuelo, who tried to hang his seven-year-old son with an electrical cord. My abuelo had almost murdered my father, too, had pushed my abuela's face through walls and thrown his sons like empty bottles against the kitchen floor. The Captain did not drink, as my abuelo and bisabuelo and Jon had drunk. Instead, he became a captain.

One time, when I was fifteen, he brooded over dinner. We had just listened to a radio program on addiction. *Why don't they just stop?* he said, and dropped his fork, which struck against his plate a furious note. He said it with the force of a man who has been robbed, as he had. The Captain never taught us Spanish because it was the language in which my abuelo had screamed.

I flinched as that note rang out from his plate, but kept quiet. I hadn't found heroin yet, but I had already betrayed myself. I knew that to stop was not always an option. And that the longer you went, the harder it got. Self-knowledge didn't save you, it only made it hurt more to watch yourself.

I suspect that anyone is capable of anything under the right circumstances. We don't want to believe this. We want identity to be solid, but even science proves that it is reactive, changing all the time. We invent nothing. We are in constant collaboration with our contexts. We are more alike than we think. Not everyone has a bottomless pit, and not everyone will go to such lengths to fill it. Not everyone will use their body like a hammer, will hammer the body the way that I have. Not everyone needs to get so close to dying to find that they exist. I'm not the only one; I was just the only one at that table.

25

Amaia knew where she came from. She had been to the desert of Chile. She spoke the language of her grandparents. She still attended her childhood Catholic Church. Before meals, she prayed, and she knelt between my legs like it was another kind of prayer. What I mean is, she didn't question what was hers.

When she asked about Jon, I said the same things I'd been saying my whole life. I listed the objects in that small suitcase. *So what that he's an alcoholic*, she said. *Aren't you curious? That's still part of you.* I thought about this. Somehow, I'd never thought about it before, or had been having the same thought for thirty years. Something had prompted me to contact my half sister, though it didn't feel like curiosity. That act had felt strangely drained of emotion. All I had felt that day, and every day since, was for Amaia. She had, it seemed, become the receptacle, the provocateur of all my feeling. Though I knew that impulse to meet my sister had meant something. I knew I did not always feel things at the site of their provocation.

I'd done this kind of detective work before, scrutinized my actions to determine how I'd felt. *You're so brave!* people had said to me after my first book was published. But I wasn't brave. Scrutinizing my life was the only way I could make sense of it. And writing was the only way I could think clearly. The thoughts in my mind ran on a loop—they were worried, obsessed, and small. They went nowhere. By building a story, I could find a beginning, middle, and end.

When she asked me if I was curious about Jon, I paused. I knew that my blind spots could be gaping. That other people could be mirrors, if you trusted them. I trusted her, didn't I?

I looked at the suitcase that had held the four or five things I knew about Jon. Suddenly, it grew so heavy. Then, it was no longer a suitcase. It was a warm, beating thing. I followed its sinews, the blue rivers of its circulatory system, and I found that it led back to me, to my body. Thirty years ago, a child had decided that I didn't need it. And it was true; I hadn't needed it. I had been getting around just fine on one leg.

You weren't ready before, she said. *Now you're ready.*

26

In Iowa, I waited for the hotel shuttle bus. Then I waited in the hotel lobby, sipping tiny cups of lemon water while I waited for Amaia. My mother called and I did not answer. Amit called and I did not answer. My body ached from no sleep. I stared at the same page of a book for an hour. Every time the lobby door spun around, I looked for her.

When she finally appeared, face flushed from the cold and cocktails, I sprung up.

My girl, she said, so sweetly. She leaned over me, hair falling all around, and kissed me all over my face. *I love you*, she said.

After her lecture, a crowd of young women gathered around her, stars in their eyes. I sat in the front row of seats, now empty, and watched her talk to them. She was a wonderful speaker. I waited, and began to feel a little awkward. The host of the event sat beside me. She held a computer in her lap and on it were pictures of her cat. I leaned over and *awwwed*. She showed me more pictures, and, grateful for someone to talk to, I told her about my dog.

As the host drove us back to the hotel, I reached from the backseat and squeezed Amaia's shoulder. She pulled away from me. My hands, though cold, began sweating.

What's wrong? I asked her once we returned to the hotel room. I stood at the foot of the bed. She lay on the bed, staring at her phone.

Nothing, she said.

Not nothing, I said. *Please tell me.*

We can talk about it later, she said.

Please, I said. *Tell me now.*

You didn't have to do that, she said.

Do what? I asked.

Humiliate me.

What? I said. My body went cold with sweat all over.

You were supposed to be there with me, she said. I had been flirting with the host, she said. I told her I had not. I was sure that I had not. I had been glad for someone to talk to, but there was a difference. I knelt on the bed and reached for her. She pushed me away.

There's something in you, she said. *I don't trust it. You need people to want you.*

No, I insisted. My hands shook. I told her that maybe that had once been true of me, but not for a long time.

Loyalty is important to me, she said. *We might just be different in this way. It doesn't mean there's anything wrong with you.*

I love you, I said. *Please trust me.*

I'm afraid I will never be enough for you, she said. *My love will never be enough to satisfy you. You need more.*

I knew she was wrong—the idea that I could want anyone else while I wanted her this much was insane, laughable. But as I lay next to her, I felt that old shame slip into me. I was inappropriate and over-sexual. I did not see myself clearly. I had humiliated her.

Pandora's jar isn't mentioned until Hesiod's later work— "Works and Days"—in which she has a name. Her name means "all-gifted," though her gifts mean nothing in the end. She wears a garland crown from the Horae, fine gowns from Athena, and the Charites adorn her in jeweled necklaces. But this Pandora also wears Aphrodite's gift of "a cruel longing and cares that weary the limbs." Here, Hesiod also gives her the jar of ruin. Does Pandora even know what is in her jar?

Jars are meant to be opened. Her creator gave it to her, and she opened it. Of course she did. Everything flew out— and who else was there to blame? Pandora must have also blamed herself—she had no memories, no history, just those beautiful gifts, just that jar. A later, more accurate translation of her name revises its meaning to "all-giving." In the end, she has nothing. She stands amid her ruined world with only *Elpis*, hope, like a butterfly on the lip of her empty jar.

I lay there all night, waiting for her to touch me. *If she touches me*, I thought, *I will be okay.*

Please, I said.

Go to sleep, she said, and turned her back to me.

As the sun rose, brightening the drawn curtains, I was hardly anything left—just a glowing sliver of shame. I didn't care if she was right or wrong.

I'm sorry, I whispered.

Come here, she said, and folded me in her arms.

27

The drive from Brooklyn to Torrington, Connecticut took three hours. Three hours, and thirty years. I planned to buy flowers once there, rather than let them wilt in the car. I also suspected I'd want the extra time to find my feet in a strange town, to locate the impulse that brought me there. When I woke that morning in Brooklyn, soaked with sweat, I felt nothing.

The first leg of the trip is along Interstate 95, the same I take to Massachusetts to see my mother. Gliding down the freeway, I turned up the stereo's volume, my finger tapping across the radio keys. I filled the car with soaring pop music. That's all I'd been able to listen to for months. I beat the heel of my palm against the steering wheel to the pulse of these love songs. My phone chimed from the passenger seat, echoed by a clang in my chest, Amaia's touch firing across the 2,500 miles between us, ringing that bell. Only she knew where I was going, and I imagined her hands cupping my buzzing body, carrying me outside, releasing me like a caught bee.

After Stamford, the city seeped out of the landscape. On a smaller highway, the road emptied, its surface bleached and pitted with potholes. I switched lanes, switched radio stations, noticed my palms wet on the wheel.

When signs for Torrington appeared, I slowed. Off the exit, the trees thinned, replaced by squat houses, their vinyl siding faded to pastels. I parked outside a strip of shops and opened a smudged glass door that read PHARMACY.

Hallmark makes no card for this occasion. I owed no *Thank you*. No *Love*. No *Condolences*. *Get Well Soon?* Not likely. I bought one with a puppy on the cover and a blank inside and asked the clerk where to buy flowers.

Real flowers? She shook her head slowly. *Maybe at the Stop & Shop? Toward Manchester?*

It is a former mill town, but the last mill was shut down after Torrington was devastated by hurricanes in 1955, and the town never stood up again. It has the grim set of all such towns, reminds me of the Rust Belt city where I taught for one year—pawn and tobacco shops with a few ghosted stares from inside. Endless salt- and ice-crusted winters. Gas station coffee drinkers, the few faces leaning over the Lotto counter white and textured by smoke and sorrow. People with bodies slanted like they've been walking against the wind their whole lives, because they have.

When I parked and walked across the lot of another dilapidated plaza, headed for the *Grocery*, a cluster of women with puffy coats and eyes fell silent and watched me, heads turning, eyes sharp, chins tilted upward.

Real flowers? asked the man behind the Keno machine.

I nodded, the only other man in the store watching me, slack-jawed, a pale slice of belly hanging over his jeans. I smiled at him. I wanted to go home, to drive back to my apartment in Brooklyn, where I could look at my things and remember who I was.

At the Stop & Shop toward Manchester, I picked out a garish bouquet and a bag of truffles. I joined a checkout line behind a father and his small son.

You go first. The father smiled at me. *We're still deciding.* He gestured at the boy, who considered the candy display with furrowed intensity. I smiled and thanked him, not because I was late, but because his boy was the first unbroken thing I had seen all morning.

The house sat at the end of a road, stout and gray, wearing a disheveled skirt of porch. I glided toward it, turned off the radio, and wiped my palms on my thighs, one at a time.

As I turned into the driveway, a man stepped out onto the porch. I hated arrivals. When the engine died, something died in me, too. Or woke. *You're like a train*, Amaia said so often. *Like a shark. You never stop moving.*

The man took a step toward the porch railing. Hands on the wheel, I closed my eyes and inhaled, the seatbelt pressing against my chest. *Please*, I thought, *stay there.* I just needed a few more breaths before I faced him.

When I opened my eyes, he stood on the other side of the

car door. I had been imagining his face for days, but I could not look at him. I threw my vision out of focus, blurred his edges. My chest clenched, released a cool spray of fear into my shoulders, throat, and lungs. Ears burning, I smiled, and unclasped the seatbelt. There was nowhere to go but out. I gathered the flowers and my purse from the passenger seat.

He stood so close to my door that I waved him back so that I could open it. Behind his glasses, his eyes grasped at me. There were two panes of glass between us, and they were not enough. I opened the door and stepped onto the leaf-papered ground, into the cold afternoon, and faced him.

Hello, he said, and then my name. Everything about him, but worst of all my name in his mouth, stung—bright as a fingertip on a skinned knee. I embraced him, if you can embrace someone without touching them. My face so near his stubbled cheek, I felt him tremble, smelled aftershave and alcohol. We stood in the leaves and he did not invite me into the house until I gestured toward it. Then I followed him through the back door, the yellowed pantry, into the kitchen.

Two women sat at a folding table. He stepped back, presenting me. I handed the flowers to the younger woman, who bore a close resemblance to him, and I think, to me. She had tan skin and sea-glass eyes, and her hands shook as she took the bouquet.

Look! she said to the older woman, who was very old. *Real flowers!*

The older woman stared deafly at the flowers, at me, at Jon.

This is her, Jon shouted. I flinched.

What? she asked. She squinted and smacked her gums. She had no front teeth, and leaned her speckled forearms on a crossword puzzle.

THIS IS HER, he shouted again.

She stared, having heard but not understood.

LYNN'S DAUGHTER, he added.

She tilted her head, understanding finally. She clapped her withered hands one time. *Then she's your daughter, too!* she said, grinning, her tongue tucked in the space where her front teeth had been.

Yes, he nodded, smiling back at her, at me.

No, I thought.

28

In his confessions, St. Augustine asks God "why tears are so sweet to the sorrowful." Euripides, in *The Trojan Women*, asks, "How good are the tears, how sweet the dirges? I would rather sing dirges than eat or drink." I, too, have always had a taste for tears. I was a colicky baby and an emotional child. I cried for *The Fox and the Hound*, for baby birds in our backyard, for bullied classmates on the school bus. Most of all, I cried when the Captain left. I watched him walk away again and again, and I sobbed, thinking *Come back, come back*. I hugged my crying mother and thought, *I will do anything*.

When he was gone, I kept a close watch on my mother, who was good at hiding her loneliness, but not good enough. Some days, a panic gripped me that she would never return from the grocery store. I stared at the driveway, *Come back, come back*. I called her from friends' houses, *Pick up, pick up*.

The first movie I ever saw in a theater was Disney's *Bambi*. Bambi's father—the Prince of the Forest—is more myth than presence. He leaves the young Bambi virtually orphaned when Bambi's mother is killed by hunters. When Bambi's mother died, I was inconsolable. I was three years old and I recognized the breadth of his loss. I knew there were kinds of despair howling enough to fell a forest.

I decided I needed to toughen up when I turned eight. On the bus, on the way home from school, I imagined each of my family members dying. When tears rose in my eyes, I suppressed them. *You can't cry*, I told myself. *Or they really will die.*

Around the same time, I realized that my parents would not always be around to make me brush my teeth. Like most children, I did not want to brush my teeth. But even then the idea that I would be lost to the whims of my own desires scared me. I lay in bed and told myself: *You will not be able to sleep unless you brush your teeth.* I repeated this mantra until it became rote, an induced obsession. It became true. I could not sleep unless I brushed my teeth. I still cannot.

Most importantly, I stopped crying when the Captain left. I didn't have to try—I just stopped. In fact, I barely remember his departures after the age of eight. When my mother cried, I wrapped my arms around her, dry-eyed.

After I stopped crying, I became clumsy. I tumbled down stairs and walked into walls. I tripped *up* stairs and burned my hands on the stove. I cut my fingers while chopping vegetables and once gave myself a paper cut on my eyeball. A therapist once told me that extreme clumsiness in children is a sign of depression. Severely depressed people do not cry. Nor do severely neglected babies. Tears are an essentially hopeful act—inherent to them is the body's belief that someone is watching. When the psyche gives up hope that those cries will be answered, the tears stop. I was not severely neglected, nor severely depressed. But I did stop hoping for rescue. My mother begged the Captain to stop leaving. I woke from dreams calling his name. But when he was gone, he was gone. No amount of crying could summon him.

In my mid-teens, the dry spell ended. The first time I fell in love, I put my favorite PJ Harvey song on repeat and cried all afternoon. That first girlfriend and I would cry like it was a kind of lovemaking—our bodies surging together, damp and entangled. We cried to Kristin Hersh, Tori Amos, Ani DiFranco, Otis Redding, Leonard Cohen.

Real sorrow needs no soundtrack. Our tears were not crocodile, but they meant something other than sorrow. Of all my tears, these were closest to what the Romanian writer E. M. Cioran coined "voluptuous suffering," in his 1937 work *Tears and Saints*. My sobs at sixteen were sensual and sweeping—in tears, I inhabited my body with an abandon that I could not sexually, or in any other way.

Studies tell us that women are more prone to tears and melancholia, and men to anger. They tell us that we enforce these expressions of feeling by gender, that women's anger has, over centuries, been converted to tears and melancholia. The only time in thirty-two years that I expressed anger was in my early adolescence, the time during which the Captain still describes me as possessed.

During the time that I was addicted to drugs, I rarely cried. When I was high, I was high. And the increasing misery that I felt at all other times was the dry kind. Even in the far reaches of my own denial—the enormous kind necessary to pursue any so seriously life-threatening habit—I knew no one could rescue me. That I was the only person who could walk out of that mess. That the only help I could accept was God's.

29

Jon looks like the Captain. At least, he once did. When his sister, Joan, led me into her small study and handed me a stack of photographs that she had pulled from their albums, I blinked. It could have been the Captain, at twenty. The same brown skin and thick hair, the same gentle handsome face. He was beautiful. I studied his grade school pictures as I could not bear to look at Jon himself—searching. I raised their yellowed squares to my face for closer inspection and found my own face at that age—the shy gaze and heart-shaped mouth, the round cheeks and blinding innocence.

He had disappeared for a few minutes and as I examined the pictures, he returned and peered over my shoulder. I smelled his aftershave, the smoke and beer on his breath. I have always loved that combination of scents. Now, my stomach clenched. Like a hovering wasp, his nearness made my shoulder smart. It was the strongest feeling I had in that house, and the strongest reaction I've ever had to another person, except Amaia. He stood too close, stared too long, and emitted a cloying need that saturated the air like their cigarette smoke, which stung and watered my eyes.

The house was dark and cluttered with inhalers. Joan wheezed and fell into coughing fits that lasted minutes. When not speaking or coughing, she tucked a steady chain of cigarettes and antiseptic-smelling lozenges into her mouth, punctuated by puffs from an inhaler. As I looked at the photographs, she lowered herself into the nearby chair and rested her arms on a card table stacked with albums, newspaper, and a Bible.

You're even prettier than the pictures online, she said, and dropped her gaze to the Bible, pinching the threads of its tasseled bookmark. *I haven't read your book, but I mean to.*

Oh, no. Don't read my book, I insisted. *I'd rather you get to know me in person.*

She nodded, still looking at the Bible. *The past is in the past*, she said. I nodded, though the past was all around me, its yeasty breath hot on the back of my neck.

Jon grew bored when there were no more pictures of him and left to join the old woman, Pat, at the kitchen table. As I flipped through the remaining photos, a startling pair of eyes looked out at me—steady and bright as two small seas set in a serious face, the curved mouth dark with lipstick.

Who is this? I asked, holding out the photograph.

That's Edith, said Joan. *Your grandmother.*

I squinted at the image. She had all the parts of me I'd never seen on anyone else. My small, strong shape; my narrow waist and green eyes. Most of all, that look. Something soft and hard at the same time—in her body, but most of all her face, that gaze so firm and sad. It was not a quality I considered, when I considered my own qualities, but I recognized it. She was young, early twenties. Already so weary, as if she knew something she couldn't un-know. I remembered meeting her when she was dying, that wild rasp of death crawling up inside her.

The final photographs showed an older man with Joan as a girl. He had a broad face, still handsome at what must have been seventy. I saw where we all got that mouth, and our skin.

That's Pop Lightman, said Joan. *He was an Indian.*

30

Four months into loving her, I cried. Once I started, I could not stop. It was not voluptuous. It was not ecstatic. It was not sweet, except in the way that a sweet thing is a siren, its call impossible to ignore. Except in the way that a sweet thing, a thing you cannot ignore, can ravage. If *sweet* means *irresistible*, then my tears were sweet. But they were not pretty and they did not taste good.

In the past, I rarely cried over lovers. I never fought with lovers. I never waited for lovers. And I never lost control. My worst fear was to be needy. When I thought about neediness, I felt like there were snakes on me. When I thought about asking for something that someone couldn't or wouldn't give me, I felt like I had stepped in shit. Women who obsessed over men who did not give them what they needed repelled me, as if need were a contagious disease. I looked at the brokenhearted, at the needy, at the unrequited, at women who waited like my mother had waited and I thought, *never*.

In Aesop's fable of the fox and the grapes, the fox desires the grapes. The grapes, however, are out of his reach. So the fox tells himself he does not want the grapes. The grapes make him sick. He convinces himself.

When I was still a child, I had decided that grapes weren't so sweet after all. I would rather have lived in a world without the sweetness of grapes than in this world, where grapes were often out of reach, and did not lower themselves no matter how hard I cried. At thirty-two, I bit Amaia's lip. That sweet flooded my mouth and I remembered.

I often kidded about the voracious need that must be hiding deep inside me. I sat for hours in therapy sessions, searching for my feelings. I wanted to "get in touch with them." I thought that when I finally found them it would be like a reunion with a childhood friend—emotional, surely, but also sweet—a reward for all my hard work. I did not think that I was leaving messages for a serial killer. I did not think that my feelings, receiving my invitation, would arrive on my doorstep like a cabal of madwomen and refuse to leave. I thought that the host of the party decided when it ended and her guests went home. But feelings have terrible manners—they are like children, or drunks. They are mad. They gorge as the starved will gorge, until they are sick, until their stomachs split. As you or I would, if we were exiled for thirty years. They do not leave when you want them to. They leave when they are finished.

31

Later, we took our own pictures in the kitchen. Joan and Jon stood on either side of me, and I couldn't help leaning away from Jon. He felt like a burning thing: I wouldn't reach for it unless I had to.

We sat back down at the table and I showed them the pictures. Joan raised a plastic inhaler and the lips she pressed against its plastic mouth were the same Cupid's bow of my mouth, and Jon's.

Jon had not aged well. His body bloated, skin jaundiced, eyes murky in the way of lifetime smokers and drinkers. Years of use build a scrim between the addict and the world. I only saw this after I got clean. A year sober, I ran into an old boyfriend who was still using and saw it for the first time, like a smudged window between us.

In these new pictures, the resemblance between our faces was obvious, though Jon was no longer the handsome man from those old photos. He didn't look like my father. He just looked like a man with my mouth.

He seemed childlike. Simple. But underneath I sensed another Jon. A colder, more seeing Jon, someone searching. I remembered that my mother had once described him as *smart like a fox*. She had once described me in similar terms. It occurred to me that his facade might be intentional. Maybe he thought it was what *I* wanted, that I had come there looking for someone who was looking for me.

My mother, though wise in many ways, had retained a certain innocence. I had manipulated her easily when I was still a child, driven by my own desperations. She was a smart and perceptive woman, but one easily blinded by love and by her own wishes. When she met Jon, she was twenty-two. Of course she fell for that beautiful boy, so eager to say what she wanted to hear. But I was not a child. I saw the part of him that was capable of anything.

You look like your mom, he said. *How is she?*

She's great, I said.

I remember when you were born, he said. *At the cabin. Not far from here, on a lake.*

I nodded, still staring at the photo we'd just taken.

You should take her there, said Joan, watching him. Seven years older, she had spent her life watching him, watching after him.

You were born on a shower curtain, he continued. *A new one—we bought it just for you.*

I laughed at this. I knew that the shower curtain had been tucked under a sheet, over a bed. He smiled, but distantly, like someone who doesn't get the joke, or isn't listening.

I cut the umbilical cord, he said. *Your mother made me bury the placenta in the backyard.*

Wow, I said. It seemed he'd been waiting all afternoon to say these things. His voice was gentle, like pulling acorns from his pocket.

I should get going, I said, and pushed back my chair. No one argued, but I felt something retract in him, sulky. I hugged Joan and Pat.

I'll walk you out, he said.

In the driveway, he stared at me. My hand clutched the car door handle.

I've waited a long time for this day, he said. It sounded like a lie. Sometimes the hardest true things sound like lies when you say them, too. I can't always tell the difference. *I'd love to come visit you in the city*, he said. I nodded.

Maybe sometime, I said. *When I'm not so busy.* I got in the car and drove away. In the rearview, I could see him standing in the middle of the street, waving until I turned.

Thirty minutes later, I could breathe. I called Amaia.

You are brave, she said. But I didn't believe her. I had not even been able to look him in the eye.

They are sick, I told her, and described their faces, how they seemed buried inside themselves. I didn't say, *I am sick, too.* I didn't tell her, *I have what they have.* Only grace had stepped between me and that fate. Grace, and my mother. She had glimpsed that future, and driven our car in the other direction. She had been brave. She had had nothing, but she closed that door and painted over it. Jon had never come looking for me, had never called or sent a birthday card. She found me a better father. So what was I looking for?

Amaia's wife requested that she never speak to me when they were both in their house. Amaia agreed. I didn't like it, but I saw that it was fair. We had only been talking for a month, then. They had been together for eight years. I did not know how long they would continue living in the same house.

The wife was a teacher at their local elementary school. In the desert, a town is an island. The wife did not want to leave. She could not leave for at least the school year. When I tried to talk about this, Amaia went quiet. She said things like, *there's no place for us. I don't know how this can work. I'm not right for you.* She stopped answering the phone.

I cried. I curled on my bed in my now-empty apartment and cried like an animal. Humans are the only animals known to weep tears of emotion. When I say that I cried like an animal, I mean that I cried like a baby. My cries had no language, no thought, they consumed me like hunger, like sleep, like the one thing a baby knows—that love is the only thing keeping it alive. When the baby's mother leaves the room, the baby remembers this and screams. Over time, the baby learns that the mother always returns. The baby learns to soothe itself, to trust that the mother will not let it die.

Colicky babies seem slower to learn this. Even the mother's warmth cannot assuage the terror of their dependence. When I was a baby, my mother did not sleep. She had been a neglected child. She could not bear the sound of my cries. She came running every time. Finally, half-mad with exhaustion, armed with the wisdom of other mothers, she locked herself in the bathroom. I cried. I screamed the brilliant fury of the dying. In my tiny animal mind, I was dying. My mother turned on the shower, leaned her back against the bathroom door, and she cried, too.

My tears did not bring my Amaia running. She did not answer the phone. *Please answer the phone*, I texted her. *I need you.* I did not say, *I feel like I am dying*, though I did. She did not answer.

Maybe it is reductive to draw comparisons between these things. Maybe it is obvious. Psychologists have been comparing them for centuries. I had read the psychologists, just as I had read books about addiction while high on heroin. I had read books about bulimia while bingeing. All my life I have lamented the distance between what I know and what I do.

When we were together, she often adored me. She adored me with gifts, with love, with her mouth and hands. I went stupid with pleasure. I thought I had never felt so loved.

Your father was like that, my mother said, when I described it. *You and he were so close when you were little. He adored you.* I remembered. The Captain had written songs for me, had sung me to sleep and awake. Had spent hours listening to my stories, catching my baseballs, showering me with kisses. *But when he was gone*, said my mother, pausing to find the right words. *It was like he was dead.*

I never remember you crying, my mother said. *Have I ever told you that?*

I went to work, I met with friends, I ran laps around Prospect Park, but I only ever did one thing, and I never stopped: I waited.

I waited for her to call me back. I waited for her to come to New York. I waited for her wife to move out. I waited for some sign that she would stay. Each day, the waiting blotted out more of everything else. My memory went patchy. My hands went shaky. I texted her through entire meals with Amit. Through entire movies, classes, and six-hour drives. Every time I opened the apartment door, I wished for her to be on the other side of it.

Once, I walked out of a classroom in the middle of my own lecture to take her call.

Once, I crashed into a parked car while staring straight ahead, my mind gone.

She's worth it, Amit said. *You're worth it.* But increasingly, when I told Amit about the wife, how they still stayed in the same hotel room, went to church and family dinners together, she got a funny look. I knew what she was thinking: *never.* I would have thought the same thing.

33

My sweet wild girl,

You are off on your journey. My brave girl. My curious girl. My girl whose burning heart will not be satisfied by the easy thing. You, mi amor, are an unusual girl. I am grateful that you are rushing through my life right now.

This time, I stopped in downtown Brooklyn on my way out of town and bought three Nets T-shirts. Pat had devoured the truffles I'd brought, murmuring happily as she unwrapped them with her knotty hands, so I picked up some miniature cheesecakes at Junior's.

My mother had explained that Pat was essentially the widow of my great aunt, Camille, whom they called Mina. In the interim between my visits, Joan had filled in the details.

Pat and Mina had been childhood best friends in the 1930s until Pat's family moved to another town. Both had married men in their twenties, then reunited when they coincidentally ended up employed by the same doorknob factory. They worked at that factory for the rest of their careers, and lived together for the rest of Mina's life. Together, they had traveled the country, and, I gathered, been the emotional caretakers of Joan and Jon, whose father and mother were indisposed by alcoholism and anger, respectively.

Joan was a devout Baptist and she described Pat and Mina's relationship in careful words. It must not have been easy to navigate that tacit acknowledgement in a way that honored her affection for them, her religious faith, and what I'm sure she already knew of my own sexual proclivities. As a younger woman, I might not have been capable of appreciating that complexity, or responding in language that mirrored hers. I knew little of my motivations for having sought her out, but I knew that they did not include challenging the delicate balance of her values. I was grateful to have already learned that opposing beliefs can rest in the minds of not a few, but most people, myself included.

Amaia's family did not overtly acknowledge her relationship, though her wife was a part of her family and participated as such. They simply did not name it. Socialized in my mother's post-sixties feminist worldview, I once would have found this outrageous. I had named my bisexuality before I ever kissed a girl. Luckily, experience had humbled me before I met Amaia.

Pat's story moved me. And Joan's ability to accept and even revere their love moved me. It was easy to be curious about them, to access empathy for their lives and limitations. Their vulnerabilities did not repel me, as Jon's did. Speeding down Interstate 95 that gray morning, I already dreaded his close smell, braced myself for the soft scalpel of his gaze. His effect on me was shocking. Though it discomfited me, the strength of it was also magnetic. I have long known that loathing is nearly always a symptom of self-recognition. And I knew even then that I was not looking for him so much as myself.

34

In my last year of college, I took a job as a dominatrix. At work, I dressed in nurse uniforms, in police uniforms, in fishnets and corsets like a saloon prostitute in an old western. Men paid me to be a mother, a maid, a customs officer, a nurse, a sadist. Sometimes, they paid to hurt me. They paid to want. Doctors, lawyers, janitors, teachers, politicians, husbands, soldiers, holy men and criminals, they brought it to me. They begged. They crawled across floors. They wept. They grasped at my ankles and howled with hunger. They were ecstatic with want, sainted with want, bodies writhing and cringing, burning up on pyres of want, grasping at the wet wick of my body.

When I was twenty-two, I saw a woman suspended from a ceiling by hooks dug through the flesh of her back. We were at a party in Manhattan. She went by the name Lola, and I Justine—my namesake the Marquis de Sade's famous submissive heroine. In a rubber dress and stilettos, I stood on a staircase of a warehouse in Chelsea and tilted my head back. Lola's eyes at half-mast, her face was beatific, body glittering with makeup and pearly sweat. The stainless steel hooks gathered and lifted the skin over her shoulder blades in two mounds. All 120 pounds of her hung from those two handfuls of flesh. The puncture wounds wept, but Lola did not. Her body glowed with the pain, as if electrified— as if Electra, brilliant with relief, with glory, with revenge, with *kathartikos*. She was beautiful. I looked up at her and imagined my younger self, at eleven or twelve years old, standing beside me on that staircase, all those leathered bodies writhing below us. *Look*, I imagined saying to that girl.

Later, when I remembered this, I understood it as a desire to annihilate my own innocence. I had conjured the child in me at her most hurting age and I showed her something shocking, incomprehensible. I wanted to break that innocence, so that she would never be shocked again.

Now, I think different. It was a tender impulse, not a violent one, and what I showed her was not incomprehensible. I don't know what hoisted Lola up to those rafters, but I know she chose it. I know that she glowed like a planet, radiated light and gravity, colors like cosmic gases colliding, her body ringed as Saturn. When they lowered her, she was just a woman. Her face, slick with sweat, was softer than I had ever seen it, as if she'd just been born. Black hair wet against her forehead, she smiled at me, touched my face with her hot hand.

The Catholic monks of Opus Dei, like their thirteenth-century predecessors, practice self-flagellation in prayer. In India, Pakistan, Iraq, and Iran, some Shiites march in parades, practicing their versions—*zanjeer zani* and *tatbir*—sometimes with knives, blades, and chains. In Chinese medicine, coins are dragged across the body until blood rises to the surface in great striping hickeys. This treatment, *cao gio*, literally translates to "catch the wind," and is believed to treat "wind illness" and restore the body's balance. In this country, some teenage girls cut themselves with knives and scissors and few of them describe the urge as one to punish.

By the time I looked up at Lola, I had spent hours under tattoo guns, had slid poison needles into my arms, had shoved my own hand down my throat, had flung my body at so many perilous things, but I had never wanted to die. I was not a masochist. What I mean is, the difference between what is holy and what is pathological is sometimes a matter of fashion. What I mean is, maybe I already knew that my own healing would never look like a laying of hands, not the gentle kind. Maybe I wanted to spare that girl the extra hell of believing she was broken. We are all broken. And repair often hurts. And the ways we find to fix ourselves do not always look like fixing. Sometimes they fail, but they are never wrong.

35

Since my last visit to Connecticut, a cousin had written me. Joan had given her my e-mail.

What do you remember? I asked her. The cousin remembered her mother's stories about walking with Pop in Hartford and the white men who glared at him. *He was dark, you know*, she said. *Indians were treated the same as blacks in the fifties. His kids didn't like to talk about it.* Nobody liked to talk about it.

The cousin belonged to a group of native descendants and wanted to find pictures of our ancestors in traditional dress, so that she could dress accordingly at their gatherings. I did not mention how unlikely I knew this was.

Not long before Mina died, the cousin heard that she had been researching our family history. When the cousin contacted Mina and asked what she'd found on the native side, my aunt refused to show her anything. *She wasn't happy,* the cousin told me. Mina stopped corresponding with her.

An afternoon of my own research led me to a 1935 census. In the small empty box indicating ethnicity, Pop had scratched a single word: *Polish*.

Why should this dead stranger's hand move me? What did I know of his shame? I had seen nothing but a few photographs. But when I read his smudged script, I tasted the word—*Polish*—and my lips drew the kiss of that *p*, my tongue tucked through the ring of *o*. I might have licked the page, if there'd been one. His small lie—a seed in the shook rattle of me.

Research was easier than sitting next to Jon. But the document on my computer screen smeared a stripe of that same feeling in me. That word carried something I saw in

Jon—maybe the very thing that blurred his edges, that clenched my chest when I looked at him. We all knew the impulse to erase oneself, the dark smudge it left behind.

At the kitchen table, Joan and Jon and I picked at our sandwiches as Pat devoured her cheesecake. *Mmmm*, she muttered, licking her lips. When we laughed, she laughed too, raining graham cracker crumbs on the tablecloth.

She cried all the time, Joan said. *After Mina died.* Eight years previous, Pat had come to live with them, and for months she sobbed all night, begging her to come home. When Joan woke her in the mornings, Pat remembered and wept again, asking, *Why did she leave me here? How can I go on without her?*

I stared at her working jaw, her gaze cast out the kitchen window.

She's happy now, said Jon. *As long as she has her sweets. As long as she gets to the casino once in a while.*

Ssshh, said Joan. *Don't let her hear you. She'll be bothering us to take her.*

When I asked about Pop Lightman, Jon leaned closer. *First, it was Light Man*, he said, *but Pop changed it, because*

Indians weren't really citizens. Someone, he claimed, told him about a reservation.

I nodded. I didn't tell him that Lightman was a name brought here from England, that the natives had taken, or been given white names, that there was nothing light about it. I didn't tell him that according to a 1930 census, we were Polish. I didn't tell him that no Wampanoag tribe was recognized by the Bureau of Indian Affairs until 1974, and that the tribe Pop had most likely descended from was still unrecognized.

I'd be happy to take Pat to the casino sometime, I said to Joan.

Oh, she'd like that, she said. *But I might have to go with you—she doesn't like to be separated from me for long.* She brought a hand to her mouth and began coughing.

Jon shifted in his chair, agitated at the change in subject. When her cough quieted, he spoke. *You wouldn't mind going yourself, either, would you?*

Joan smiled at me, unembarrassed. *I used to have a problem with the casinos,* she said.

Sometimes, you still do, Jon reminded her.

It was bad a few years ago, she continued. *It was a dark time for me. I started taking pills, speed pills.* She stared at her hands. *I don't think they even make them anymore.* She half smiled. *I used to hide them in my knitting.*

She used to smoke a lot of pot, too, Jon added. *Half an ounce a day!*

I'd done some things I regretted, Joan said.

But then she found Jesus, said Jon with a grin. *And became a holy roller.* He mocked her for my benefit, but she just smiled, perhaps knowing that I was an unlikely candidate to judge her.

36

On a wet weekend in early spring, Amit and I packed our computers and drove to the Cape, as we sometimes did to write for a few days at the kitchen table of my childhood home. As usual, I was waiting for Amaia to call me. When stuck or distracted, I often circle around my work, looking words up in the *Oxford English Dictionary*. On Saturday, as Amit typed across the table, I looked up the word *abandon*.

From the French, *abandoner*, "to give up, surrender (oneself or something), to give over utterly, to yield utterly." Derived from a French phrase, *Mettre sa forest à bandon*, which meant to give up one's land for a time, hence the later connotation of giving up one's rights for a time. *Etymologically, the word carries a sense of "put someone under someone else's control."*

I snorted, and Amit looked up from her computer. *What?*

I read her the entry. She smiled. *Aba means* father *in Hebrew*, she said.

I checked my phone for missed calls. Nothing. My waiting was a wire fence that buzzed softly at my back, flexing the smallest muscles there.

Abandon led me to *Abaddon*, which the internet told me appeared in the Hebrew Bible as both a place of destruction and an angel, a duality that seemed to mirror the meanings of *abandon*. That place of destruction takes the form of a "bottomless pit." In Revelation 9:11 of the New Testament, Abaddon is described as "The Destroyer" and "The angel of the abyss." Though in some religious texts, the name is synonymous with the Devil, in more cases, he is the angel who destroys at God's bidding. He is the holy destroyer.

I knew well that God's work was sometimes that of breaking. But I still did not want to break. I did not want to *mettre ma forest à bandon*, and let her chop me down. But in each moment, more than anything, I wanted her to call me. Every minute that I waited, my need grew, until I felt only the hum of that fence, the growing current in my arms and legs, my blurred vision.

When the phone finally rang, I ran to the bedroom.

It was not her. It was the wife. In a voice sweet and split as the purple skin of a plum, she told me, *You are hurting someone.* She meant herself. *I just want you to know what you are doing. You are destroying something.*

When did it start? she asked me. *What did she tell you about us?*

I said nothing.

You are evil, she told me, her voice rising. *You are a bad person. You are disgusting.*

I hung up the phone. My hands shook. I blinked at the carpet. But I did not cry.

The wife, I knew, was the real abandoned. I had surrendered something, had abandoned myself to another power. But no one had left me yet. While I felt the grief of being left each minute that she did not call, elsewhere in me I knew that she would call. What kept her from me was not a lack of desire. And maybe, somewhere, I knew even then that she would never leave me, no matter how quiet she went. But the wife was living my nightmare. She had begged her beloved to stay and her beloved was leaving. For a moment, my heart broke for her, instead of for myself. Maybe *I* was the destroyer, the angel of the abyss that had swallowed all three of us.

Maybe I was evil. Why was I holding on so tightly? I knew that if I let go it would be easier for everyone. I would have if I could.

Joan's previous house had burned in a fire. They'd lost almost everything, though much of Mina and Pat's belongings were still boxed in the basement.

I had expected to descend the musty stairs alone, but when I rose, so did they, and in a slow procession we all staggered into the cellar, Joan's arm hooked through mine, and Pat's weight leaned on Jon. Joan's breathing had worsened since my last visit, and when we reached the cement floor, she lowered herself into an old rocking chair, wheezing too heavily to speak. I dragged another chair beside hers and brushed off its seat. Jon guided Pat into it, his hands steady and patient as she adjusted herself, settling like an old cat on a blanket, whispering softly to herself. Observing this small tenderness, I felt a flicker of warmth for him.

Before this audience, Jon and I began to open boxes. We swiped cobwebs from our faces and snorted as dust rose from the ancient cardboard. I was looking for Mina's papers, the research she might have saved despite unwelcome findings. With each folder I spotted, hope swelled in my chest, punctured each time by stacks of yellowed receipts, invoices, and pay stubs from the doorknob factory.

Across the floor, Jon held up an old teddy bear, a moth-chewed coat, a squash racket.

Whatcha got there? Pat asked him about each. *Whatcha got there?* It was easy to imagine them fifty years earlier, that little boy craving her gentle attention.

A set of hot curlers, a box of shoes, a crate of records. A chalky coating of disappointment in my mouth. I would not find what I was looking for. As the tension of that desire slackened, I looked around, my vision sharper focused. The two women in their chairs. The bare light bulbs hung above us. And Jon, hunched over a box of old albums, in a buttoned shirt printed with guitars, thick glasses sliding down his nose.

Fear washed through me. Hot under the arms and hairline, hands tingling, heart racing as if I'd woken and found myself in a strange basement, surrounded by sad strangers, as if my whole life had been a dream from which I was now waking. I looked down at my big hands curled around a yellow sweater that I let fall back into its box.

I thought of Edie's big hands in that picture, the sad seas of her eyes, and as I breathed, I pulled it all into me—the thick smell of that basement, the oily film of Jon's lies, Pat's grief, the knowledge that I had come here looking for something and found nothing but these broken people, who were my people.

For a terrible, senseless moment I believed that we would never leave that basement, that maybe I never had, that the only true things were the things I'd tried to erase, and that now, finally, had claimed me.

Jon said my name. I looked up at him, startled. My name has always startled me, like finding a familiar face on a foreign street, in a strange basement, in a stranger's mouth, a mouth that resembles my mouth. *Look at this*, he said.

In his lap, a water-stained photo album, its stiff cover opened to the first page. Pat and Mina in front of palm trees, in front of houses, in front of a mechanical bull—each photo neatly captioned. *Grand Canyon 1950. Carlsbad Caverns 1950.* Pat in a cowboy hat. Mina in the same hat. Mina holding a prop guitar.

Bermuda 1951. A picture of Pat and Pop, seated on a porch bench. He wore a collared shirt, she a smile. Then, Mina and Pop on a beach, this one in color, both of them squinting, his face dark as wood. Another of Mina and Pop, seated under a patio umbrella, Pop indeed dark as a black man. Bermuda. How ironic to have brought her Wampanoag father to that island where his people had been enslaved, where a cohort of them still lived.

On the next page, Mina smiled up at me, her body hidden behind a wooden cutout of a man's body. Cartoonish knobby knees and ribs, a Tomahawk tucked in his breechcloth. *Mohawk Trail 1952.*

I thought of Emily Dickinson's *Master Letters*—those

mysterious love letters found in her papers, never sent. To a lover, to God, to the devil—we'll never know. Unlike her poems, they are plaintive with longing, with submission to her unnamed Master. My favorite lines: *I've got a Tomahawk / in my side but that / dont hurt me much, / [If you] Her Master / stabs her more- / Wont he come to her- / or will he let her seek him.* How alike is the longing for love and the longing for our hidden selves. If Jung is right, then there is no difference at all.

Next was a photograph of Pat, her small face atop the wooden shape of a massive woman's body, long black braids falling over her enormous breasts. *Mohawk Trading Post, Shelburne, Mass.*

Next, a cluster of teepees. *Wigwam Motel, Gallup New Mexico.* On the opposite page, Mina wore a feathered headdress and stood between a man and woman in native dress, their faces dark as her father's. *Real Indians 1950.* I squinted at the picture, and almost laughed. *Real Indians?* This woman, unwilling to acknowledge her own native blood, on a tour of native lands, posing for pictures with *Real Indians*.

Me at twenty, in shooting galleries, so sure that I was different from those junkies, so sure that I had a choice. Me in the dungeon, drunk on strangers' desire, sure I was different from every woman there. Me, never crying when the Captain left, never chasing anyone, believing I was immune to abandonment. I believed in free will. I believed in reinvention. *Look how close I can stand to the fire and not become it.* Unable to admit the truth: I was already burning.

38

All the kids were doing it. That's what I told my mother when I came home from fifth grade with a bloody hand. I didn't actually see any other kid do it. I already felt like Houdini— with the right pants, a baggy T-shirt, I could disappear myself. What else could I do with that body, all the things that it wanted? Those boys dared each other, pointing that eraser, an accusation of softness, of the wrong kind of want. The Faggot Test, they called it. *Prove it*, they said to each other. I grabbed it. They hadn't even seen me standing there. I pressed the pink tip against the back of my hand and scrubbed. Bits of rubber and skin peeled away, left a burning white stripe, beaded with blood.

Erasure is never simple. Whack the mole and another one pops up behind you. Scrub the page or the skin or the census, draw the curtain and you don't disappear, you only replace yourself with darkness. Hide a body and the harder it will fight to remind you what it feels. The longer you starve it, the hungrier it gets.

I rubbed my skin until it screamed. *Why did you do that?* my frightened mother asked me. What could I have said? *I am trying to beat back this body, to feel only the things that I choose.* She thought I wanted to hurt myself, but I wanted to spare myself that greater hurt. I was only practicing. *It's nothing*, I said.

39

The final pages of Pat and Mina's album began with the heading, *Cape Cod, July & August 1952*. A house with a thatched roof. *Early Pilgrim Dwelling, Plymouth*. Then, Pat, on the steps of a familiar stone tower. *Pilgrim Monument, Provincetown*. A plaque from inside the monument. *Society of* Mayflower *Descendants 1878*. Mina atop the tower, against the black guardrails, the bay rippling below her. Mina, on the fence of a small church. *The Little Church that was So Peaceful*.

As a teen, my friends and I would skip class and drive to Provincetown. We ogled the men in their miniature shorts and rolled down the dunes, stoned silly. There were dunes in every Cape town—we went to P-town because it was queer, because *I* was queer, though that word didn't mean what it means today. My mother was queer, too; her most significant relationships after my parents' separation had been with women. But among my peers, I was an anomaly. Not an outcast, but I knew my difference and always had. As a teen-ager, I didn't know about Provincetown's history—the site of the Pilgrim's first landing, the early whaling capital, a gay haven by the beginning of the twentieth century—but I knew a part of me eased there.

By the time Pat and Mina visited in 1952 there were already drag shows. I wondered if they had gone. I wondered if they had felt, after decades of unacknowledged partner-ship, the same ease that I had felt more than forty years later.

In this country, if we are not too poor or too dark, we are allowed the fantasy of self-invention. This country was predi-cated on that fantasy. Mina didn't want to be a queer Indian girl. Who could blame her? She passed like all those other white people, posed next to the Real Indians, with her best friend Pat.

I did blame her, a little bit, crouched on that basement floor.

40

The wife had read all of our correspondences, Amaia told me. She had cut up Amaia's clothes with kitchen scissors and smashed all the gifts that I'd sent.

What had you told her? I asked. It seemed like a strong reaction from someone who already knew about us, but I did not say this.

I already told you, she said.

I'm sorry, I said.

I need some time, she said.

What kind of time? I asked, panic whirring in my chest.

I can't do this, she said.

41

Joan's church resides in the town where she and Jon were raised. On a spring Saturday, I picked her up in Torrington, the Connecticut air furred with pollen, smelling of green and dirt. We wound through small towns like hers, farmland and woods stretched between clumps of houses, each with a church, a two-pump gas station, a liquor store with a hand-painted sign. Purse clutched in her lap, she told me about her pastor. A lozenge clicked against her teeth, its menthol scent filling the car.

The pastor had been diagnosed with cancer, she said, and the doctors only gave him a few months to live. She prayed and prayed for him, the whole church did, and, *One day, he woke up—cured.* She turned to me and opened her fingers like a fast flower to indicate the magic trick of his recovery. *He has twin daughters*, she said. *They are* ... she can't remember, *not Cambodian, but—*

Filipino? I guessed.

Yes, that. Oriental. They sing during the service. Her favorite was "Jesus, What a Friend to Sinners."

Joan squeezed her inhaler, gasped its chemical mist into her wasted throat. I stopped at a minimart and bought her a bottle of water. *Thank you*, she said, wheezed, and took a small sip.

My husband used to drink, she said. *Like Jon. A little ice, splash of Coke, and gin. Mostly gin.* One night, she said, he didn't come home until early morning. Crawled into bed like a ghost, wearing only a hospital johnny. When he refused to explain, she called the hospital. He'd flown through the windshield of their car, the nurse said. Received twenty-five stitches in his head and chin. He had fought the doctor who'd tried to wire his jaw. He wasn't welcome back at that hospital, the nurse said.

Joan shrugged. *I took pills. I couldn't feel a thing. I was just*—she squinted at the road ahead—*nothing. I committed adultery.*

The first time I came to church, she said, *I was dead inside.*

42

Every morning of the first week, I woke blank as a baby. Then I remembered and my body curled in like a touched spider. I cried. I waited for her to call. She did not call. I thought of Pat, rocking herself to sleep, waking to the memory of her lost beloved. Was our love like their love? Amaia had drawn it that way. *I want a forever love*, she had often said to me. *But I don't know if you can be loyal to me.*

I called Amit.

I can't do this, I said. *I cannot stand another day of this.*

You can, she told me. *You can.*

It is as bad as I've always feared, I said.

This is not the thing you've feared, Amit said. She was right. My fear was of being unloved. Being left was only half of it. But what did it matter, if it felt as bad as I'd always feared?

Feelings are not facts, they used to say in my meetings, and it was true. But facts had never rescued me and feelings had done their work. People flung themselves off bridges and in front of trains. People ate bullets over feelings. I understood that the shore one wrecked upon was never a person. The train that barreled through me, its conductor and whistle, the flat land whose dust whirled under its wheels—they were all mine. Even that track had been laid across my body before I ever met her. Amaia was nothing but the moon whose light rode those rails, the match that lit my wick. But it didn't matter. I still burned. I did not fling myself off any bridge. But, curled on the floor of my bedroom, I understood how a person could.

When was the last time you went to a meeting? Amit asked me.

In the early months of loving her, I imagined my despair as a squall—a watery force that tossed me breathless, flooded my senses, obscured the horizon. *The stormy sea,* we called it. My therapist once suggested that I imagine a way to contain it. I closed my eyes and cupped a hand. I thought of that wild squall tossing against my palm. In that quiet room, I could hold it. But most other times it was impossible. And now? Now I canceled classes halfway through, claimed that I was ill, crying before I reached my car in the parking lot.

I had so feared her leaving. I had feared that without her I might never write again. I might never feel pleasure again. Like a magician or an alchemist she had transformed me and awoken my perfect properties. And when she left, I would lose myself. I would not see Jon and Joan and Pat ever again, because why? The desire in me that she had awoken would disappear.

At first it was true. Everything became characterized by its association to her. I hid all the letters and gifts. I deleted her name from my e-mail and phone. It didn't work. The letter *A* itself was a blade. I thought of her hands, her mouth, her voice, and doubled over. A friend sent me a Galway Kinnell poem—*Wait, for now. / Distrust everything, if you have to. / But trust the hours.*—written for a suicidal student of the poet's, but applicable to any hopeless place.

In the third week something shifted. A tiny breath. I woke up and didn't cry. I made coffee and went for a walk. I taught a class and didn't think about anything else until it was over.

That night, I got an e-mail from her—a poem by the Israeli poet Yehuda Amichai. *Forgetting someone is like forgetting to turn off the light / in the backyard so it stays lit all the next day / But then it is the light that makes you remember.*

I will wait for you, I responded.

I am not asking you to wait for me, she said.

But she also did not want me to forget, or to think that she had forgotten. A pattern emerged. Three days would pass, during which I thought of her exhaustively. On the fourth day, I would wake and take a breath. Then, I would hear from her. Sometimes a single line: *You are my Helen.* She mailed me a box of cards with the constellations drawn on them. If you held the cards to the sky, there were pinprick holes through which you could map the stars. She called me once from a town in Washington where she had traveled for work and told me about a colleague, Cristina, whom she'd met at a dinner party. *She keeps mentioning her "partner,"* Amaia said. *It made me think of you.*

43

Joan's breathing was so taxed that I had to drop her off at the church entrance before parking a few yards away. I carried her Bible inside and nodded at the ushers. The church had a carpeted floor and carpeted walls. Most of the congregants were older white folks. A few young families sat in the rear-most pews.

Early in the sermon, the pastor read from Jonah 4:1. The God of the book of Jonah first appears cruel, but is ultimately revealed to be merciful.

Jonah is the reluctant prophet. God calls him to proclaim judgment on Ninevah, and Jonah refuses. He still believes in his own will. He stows away on a ship bound for Tarshish to escape his destiny, but God calls up a mighty storm, and the ship's crew throws Jonah overboard. God's sea monster swallows him, and only in that belly does Jonah finally submit.

Jonah, whose name means *dove*, is not brave. He simply exhausts all his other choices. The only thing left to choose is God's will. And even then, after proclaiming his prophecy, Jonah shakes his fist at the Lord. His destiny does not give him peace. It enrages him. It is not what he wants. He begs God to kill him.

But God doesn't kill Jonah. God's mercy doesn't often come in the form of erasure. And the story of Jonah seems a parable of what I have often suspected—that life is a great Choose Your Own Adventure story wherein every choice leads the hero to the same princess, the same cliff. There are alternate routes, but there is only one ending, if you make it there.

I already knew that Amaia was God's storm, that every love is a sea monster in whose belly we learn to pray. But I did not know my own destiny yet, if submission meant marrying the monster, the person I became in love with her.

How shall we escape if we neglect so great a salvation? the pastor implored us. Maybe he meant: stop fighting. It's supposed to hurt. Grace is not sweet, and mercy is not getting what you want.

On Joan's first visit to the church, the preacher had looked into the congregation during his sermon and, she swore, *He looked right into me.* He asked if there was anyone present who didn't like the way they were living. Joan froze. He asked those people to raise their hands. Joan did not raise her hand. He looked right into her and said, *You can't change your life, but Jesus can.* He invited her to let Jesus into her heart.

And I did, she told me.

And he did. Jesus entered my aunt's heart and eased what hurt there. Her depression lifted. She stopped taking pills. She started taking the children to church and reading the Bible. *Everyone thought I was crazy,* she said, but when she called the preacher to tell him what had happened, he told her, *You're not crazy. You've been saved.*

That whole day I felt like a journalist, as if talking to Joan were a kind of research. I attended these visits like a job, as if I were present on behalf of some third party. But I had no outside obligation. No one even knew I was there. Even from behind it, I knew my detachment was a curtain, protecting me. I did not want to draw it back. I could not bear to step into that kitchen, that town, this church, not for real. I did not want to bring that other life, in which my heart was so broken, into this one. I needed it to remain that foggy liminal space—an emotional lobby where I'd simply taken a number and a seat. Where I was only making small talk with strangers until my number was called. I was waiting for the thing I sought to find me.

But as those two girls with the same face stood at the front of that church and sang "I'll Fly Away" so sweetly, I could see that from a few steps away, where I stood looked like no kind of waiting room. I could see that to another set of eyes, I was no interloper here, not among strangers. My broken heart was in no other building, no other body. There was only one woman, with one heart that had led her here to these people whom she had tried to erase, who had tried for generations to erase themselves. This woman had come to them, and come back again, wanting answers. This woman could not stop crying and who could blame her? From a few pews back I could see she'd spent her whole life trying to carve herself into being, to grind herself into dust, and that she sat today in this church wanting nothing more than to stop, than to be saved. But it wasn't the God of that room who was going to save me.

44

After two months, I went on a date. That is what people do after breakups, I thought. I ate lunch at a café in the East Village with a woman named Alice. Alice was so easy. Alice was sober and sexy and I knew I could never be in love with her.

A few weeks later Alice and I went to a movie. After the movie, we went back to her apartment and she showed me her guitar, her books, her plants. It was a very clean apartment. When Alice kissed me, I kissed her back. Then I began to cry.

What a lesbian, I said, half laughing. *I'm so embarrassed.*

Alice laughed, too, and handed me a tissue.

I'm a wreck, I told her.

That's okay, she said, and walked me to my car.

A few days later, I was driving to the Cape to see my mother. It was spring now, and sunlight filled the car. I rolled down the windows and turned up the radio.

My phone rang. I recognized Amaia's number and answered.

What are you doing? she asked me.

I'm driving to the Cape, I said.

I want to come to the Cape, she said.

What are you talking about? I asked her.

My wife is moving out, she said. *I want to come to New York. Can I see you?*

Of course, I said.

Alice and I had planned to go to Fire Island that Saturday. In the morning, I went to her apartment as planned. *We need to talk*, I said. *Things are not finished with my ex.*

Okay, said Alice. *I understand.*

I'm not ready to be dating you, I said.

Okay, she said again. *Do you still want to go to the beach for the day?*

I thought for a minute. *Sure*, I said.

After an hour of driving, as we neared the ferry, my phone rang. It was Amaia. I didn't answer. She called back. She called again and again. Then she texted me.

I am going to call one more time. Answer the phone.

My body went cold.

We have to pull over, I said to Alice.

Uh, okay, she said. I took the next exit and cruised into a neighborhood. On a residential street of ranch-style homes with tidy lawns, I pulled over. I got out of the car, told Alice to drive up the street, and watched her park a hundred yards away. I stood beside the curb in front of a blue house with white shutters. Birds rustled on the rim of a stone fountain in the yard and took turns in its shallow pool. I was the only person in sight. I squinted at my phone in the sunlight and paced. When Amaia called again, I answered.

What are you doing? she asked me. *Who are you with?*

No one, I said. *A friend.*

Don't lie to me, she said. *What the fuck are you doing?*

I'm not doing anything, I said. *It's not what you think.*

I want you to turn the car around and go home, she said. I'd never heard her sound like that—controlled, but barely.

She was furious. But I could also hear the break in her. The fear that never rose to her surface.

Okay, I said. My legs shook.

Alice and I drove back in three hours' worth of traffic, beach chairs clanging in the trunk. When I finally dropped her back at her apartment, before closing the door she gave me a long look and in it I saw disappointment, but also pity.

That night, I tried to explain. *You broke up with me*, I reminded Amaia. It did not help. She seemed in a trance of hurt and anger. She couldn't hang up the phone and she couldn't hear me.

How could you? she kept saying. *I pulled apart my life for you.*

I had confirmed all her suspicions of me. I was disloyal. I was dishonest. I was selfish. I did not love her. Love meant different things to us.

Panic coursed through me, but other things, too. I knew that to argue with her only made it worse, but I also knew that she was wrong.

It's not true, I said. *I know how to love. I am good to the people I love.*

I know you are, she said. *I'm just sorry I'm not one of them.*

You told me not to wait, I said.

She had not asked me to wait, she said, because real love waited—you didn't have to ask.

You broke my heart, Amaia, I said, desperate. *What was I supposed to do?*

Why are you so stubborn? she said. *You don't want to give up any control.*

I could not show her what was in me. She would not accept my truth. My recovery had taught me how to look for my part in every conflict. I couldn't change her, but I knew how to change myself. Hadn't I sworn to love her forever? I knew she was scared. Her perspective could not accommodate mine. She couldn't budge. But I could, so I did.

I'm sorry, Amaia, I said. *I was wrong. I won't ever do that again.*

How do I know? she said. *How will I ever trust you again?*

I'll show you, I said. *Please say you'll still come.*

45

This time, when I pulled up to the house, Jon was standing in the road, waiting for me. He smiled at me and raised a hand. He opened the passenger door and climbed into my car, filled it with his clean sweat smell and wet stare, his nervous childish hands smoothing his buttoned shirt.

This way, he said, pointing.

As we passed the small grocery, the old mill, the pharmacy strip mall and empty sidewalks, I felt him see it all through my eyes.

This town is ugly, he said.

It's not so bad.

The casino is that way, he pointed. *If you ever want to go. Joan only plays pennies now, so she never wins.* He laughed. *I guess we've all got something.*

I nodded.

My girlfriend? he went on. *She has to take all kinds of medicine from her doctor or she goes crazy.* His girlfriend lived in subsidized housing and Joan had told me that he stayed there when he wanted to drink hard. *We've all got something*, he said again.

What have you got? I asked, as if I didn't know.

I only drink beer now, he said. *What about you?*

I haven't had a drink in ten years.

He nodded. *I went away a bunch of times.*

To treatment?

Yeah. Didn't take.

I imagined bringing him to a meeting. I knew it was silly, but I indulged the fantasy for a few miles—a reason for being there that I could understand. What if it took, this time? A destiny for both of us. A tidy resolution.

What about meetings? I asked him.

Nah, he said. *Not for me.*

As we neared the town where I was born, the trees opened. Tobacco fields stretched in long dark acres, no soul in sight but the birds along the telephone line.

It looks exactly the same, he said, and I knew he meant not only the land we drove through but the images in his mind, those pictures he'd been carrying all my life.

What do you remember? I asked him. He turned to me, as if he'd been waiting for me to ask.

I remember everything, he said. His gaze on my cheek and neck nearly burned. *Your mother was different from anyone I'd ever met*, he said, releasing me from his stare, scanning the decrepit trees of an abandoned orchard as we passed. *All she ate was nuts and dried fruit.* I heard his smile. *She lived in a Quonset hut and the first time she brought me there she got mad because I ate the whole jar.*

Had my mother thought of him when she found my own empty jars? When she'd found the liquor bottles hidden in my dresser drawer? I'd always thought the fear on her face was of the unknown in me, the dark she didn't recognize. But maybe she had.

She didn't even have a refrigerator, he went on. There was a life meant for poor Italian girls from New Jersey, and

253

it was not the life she wanted. She was beautiful and smart and she could go anywhere.

She slept naked, he said, shaking his head, and in his smile I saw both wonder and some other knowing.

What a strange thing it was. To sit so close to a strange man. A man driven by impulse. His being was more body than anything else. I was his blood. But I was also a stranger. A woman with a body inches away from him. When he looked at me I could feel the force of it. He wanted something from me, though neither of us could name what it was. It wasn't sexual, but some kinds of want are so bare, so big, that they are not any one thing. They are anything. They are every-thing. When the mind craves something it cannot bear, the body takes on its burden. My own body had shown me this. I had fed on Amaia's body with all my starving parts. What I wanted from her I could not name, so I gorged on what I could taste.

In my last days as a dominatrix, my clients' stares had felt like Jon's. Their need was so great. But there was nothing left for me to give them. I could hardly breathe in those rooms. Once, my mother told me, she had come home from work to find Jon in her closet. He was wearing one of her dresses. *What are you doing?* she had asked him.

Nothing, he had said.

46

In her desert, the heat is so hot, the light so bright that everything else is a kind of darkness, is a kind of cold. Bones lie along the roadsides, and most people are passing through—on their way to Vegas or Los Angeles or Mexico or simply to wherever is far enough to lose what chases them. The ones who are not passing through never leave.

Before I ever went there, Amaia had described it so brokenly, the way you describe a thing that is beautiful to you, but to no one else. I had sometimes described our love that way. *It's a hard place*, she often said, early on. She hadn't known me yet and even then I could tell the desert was a proxy for herself.

I loved that desert on sight. Because it was hers and because I had fought so hard to get there, but also because it felt like a different kind of ocean. Because of the light. There is too much light in the desert to hide how easily it can kill you. "Torment belongs to the desert," Jung wrote in *The Red Book*.

Why did you turn the car around when she told you to? Amit had asked me, when I recounted the events. *You didn't do anything wrong.*

I didn't know how to answer her. It hadn't felt like a choice.

In the conversations with Amaia that followed that day, I had tried all of my tools. I explained over and over the logic of my experience. I used "'I' statements" and acknowledged my own insecurities. These methods only seemed to inflame her more.

You are, you are, you are, she said. *How could you?*

It was like trying to play catch with a wall. It was beating my head against it. So I stopped trying to speak what language of resolution I knew. I could not negotiate with her perspective, so I adopted it.

I'm sorry, I said. *I'm so sorry.* I apologized all summer. I stopped calling Amit. I went to work and came home. I waited for Amaia to call me and I always answered. When I mentioned a friend whom she didn't know and she got quiet, I stopped seeing that friend. It was easier. They were choices that I made.

Of the first summer that she spent in the Southwest, Georgia O'Keeffe wrote, "There were so few flowers. There was no rain so the flowers didn't come. Bones were easy to find so I began collecting bones . . ."

Amaia's home was all dark wood—the silver steer's skull

mounted on the wall, its tapered horns glowing in the dim like a blue flame, while everything outside blistered. In her desert, you can't leave a plastic chair outside without it melting. Every wall of her two-car garage was lined with shelves—floor to ceiling rows of plastic bins meticulously labeled in her ex's schoolteacher hand. Every time I entered it, I stomped my feet, so the snakes who might hide in poisonous coils and the spiders who hung in sticky webs out of sight would know my size. *I am here*, I stomped, so that all the ghosts would know. So that I would know.

On good mornings, she woke me and we drove through the cotton fields, crop dusters sputtering overhead. We drove across the river, our hands laced below the truck windows where no one we passed could see, the sun a tipped cup bleeding light across a tablecloth. We visited one of her neighbors, an old man who told us stories and sang us songs. We bought mounds of shaved ice drenched in syrup that dyed our mouths brilliant orange and crimson, like sunsets or fresh wounds, still cold when we pressed them together.

We never touched in front of anyone out there. Her nieces and nephews climbed into my arms and fell asleep there, not knowing what to call me, only that I knew how to hold them. When I watched her with those kids my heart nearly burst. She was kind and patient. She had so much to give them in their innocence. That was how she wanted to love, I thought—complete and uncomplicated. That was how she wanted to be loved.

The good days felt like a reward for all the hard. Maybe I had been stubborn, in trying to fight for my version of our story. Colluding with hers let me into her life, and that was what I'd wanted for so long.

Other mornings, I'd walk into the kitchen and she would glower at me. *Did you like kissing her?* she would ask. *What was it like?*

In the middle of lovemaking, she would stop, roll away from me.

I'm sorry, I would say. *Amaia, please.*

I still knew that I had done nothing wrong, at least not of the magnitude she described. I had betrayed only her perfect ideal.

The psychologist Johann Friedrich Herbart proposed the theory of "psychic mechanics," of which the term "apperceptive mass" was an integral part. Ideas gleaned from experience coalesced, he said. They became a system of logic and function. Ideas that agreed with the mass were assimilated and incompatible ideas were rejected.

There was no room for what I knew in Amaia's system of logic. Though it frustrated me, there was also an innocence to it. Sometimes, I could see her try—she *wanted* to hear me, wanted to give me what I needed. But she couldn't, as if to absorb a different reality would destroy hers.

Amaia had taken care of herself in ways no child should have to. As a grown woman, she took care of her whole family. I knew about self-sufficiency and about the terror of dependence. I knew well the way an early story sticks—how high the stakes can feel so many years later. How hard we hold the things that kept us alive. I saw our similarity, our mutual grasping for something to hold us, something that felt safe.

I stopped saying certain things, because she couldn't hear them. But they did not go away. I could feel the hardening place where I kept them.

Herbart also suggested that no psychic ideas disappeared. Rejected ideas were repressed, and waited for a compatible mass, or collected until they were strong enough to form their own.

After so many morning visits, her neighbor gave me a name: *renacuajo*.

What does it mean? I asked.

Tadpole, Amaia said.

Because you are small, her neighbor added, and raised his hands to show the small space in between.

When we were children, my brother and I would wade in the shallows of our pond, hold still as shadows, and let the tadpoles brush our ankles. We scooped them into our cupped hands, admired the dark buds of their bodies, the flutter of their translucent tails.

There were snakes in the desert. The first time I saw one, stretched out dead across the road, its rattle cut off by some earlier passerby, I thought of those snakes in Texas. I thought of the ouroboros, the snake who eats his own tail, in whom, said Jung, "lies the thought of devouring oneself and turning oneself into a circulatory process . . . [The ouroboros] slays himself and brings himself to life, fertilizes himself and gives birth to himself. He symbolizes the One, who proceeds from the clash of opposites."

47

The town where I was born was hardly a town. An out of service gas station. A windowless bar with a flickering sign.

There's the bar, said Jon.

Did you used to go there? I asked.

Oh yeah, he said. I knew that a decade earlier, I would have pulled into that dirt lot and followed him inside. We would have shared the one thing I knew I had always shared with him. But this was not that life. So I kept driving.

Here, he pointed. *It's down here.*

The narrow road was dotted with houses, rain-worn toys strewn on their scraggly lawns. Beyond them lay the lake, a bowl of gray sky, its edges smudged with trees' reflections.

This one, he said, gesturing ahead. *That's where you were born.* There was a yellow house, too new to be their old cabin. But he wasn't pointing at it anyway, he was pointing to a cluster of trees a few yards away, next to which sat a small shed— hardly bigger than a doghouse—like a miniaturized version of the real house, painted the same yellow. *They must have torn it down*, he said. *Because you weren't born in that shed.*

I laughed. It seemed like a joke. A play on the way the giants of our memories appear shrunken to our adult eyes. A tiny house in this tiny town that I'd heard about my whole life. It had always seemed mythic, my dark Atlantis, the place where my lost life had begun and ended. This was it. Had I expected my young mother to step out onto the porch in her sundress, belly swollen with me inside? Had I expected a cemetery? There was nothing. Just a lake that looked like the lake I had loved all my life. Just an empty space, a clutter of leaves like a dress I had shed before stepping into another.

I drove past it and wound down the crooked road to the public entrance of the lake. A wooden dock stretched from the shore out into the water, held up by fat wooden piles splattered with seagull shit. I parked and unbuckled my seatbelt.

Let's walk out there, I said. He obeyed me and unbuckled his seatbelt, followed me out of the car. Together, we walked to the end of the pier. Hands dug into his pockets, he lumbered next to me. He stared across the lake and pointed at the yellow dot of that shed. I laughed again and this time he laughed with me.

48

Sometimes I couldn't apologize. My own knowing bucked in me.

I didn't do anything wrong! I'd shout at her.

Stop saying that! she'd say.

We fought over who was texting so late, why I had let some man stand too close to me, why she never answered the phone or called me back when she said she would—and it had always been the same: a blaze that made my ears hurt and my mind go white. She withdrew and I swelled. I wept in her bed, in the bath, in her truck, craving something she wouldn't or couldn't give.

In the beginning, I had wanted her to love me. I had wanted her to be there when I reached for her. I still wanted that.

And in pieces, she gave it to me. But now, I wanted her to see me. To listen. She had built a myth of us, a *wunderkammer* of our love story. And all the rejected parts had collected in me. *I let you into my world*, she once wrote me, as if it were a gift I had spurned. I had entered her world. I had made her my world. But it was not enough. Of course it wasn't.

I sat in her closet and called my therapist. *Help me*, I said. *How can I change myself to fix this?* My therapist told me to dunk my hands in ice water. She told me to go for a run. When I pulled on my shoes Amaia stopped me.

You can't go outside like that, she said. *You can't be crying in the street. I live here.* We had fought in airports and hotels, in restaurants and bars, on so many streets. *Stop it*, she would say when I cried. *Not here.* So I dunked my hands in ice water. I splashed it on my face. I tied a bandana over my nose and mouth to protect me from the wind and swirling dust. I ran up into the desert like a mad bandit, eyes stung red and swollen.

For the alchemists, the ouroboros was a symbol of First Matter, the *Prima Materia*, and like their similar image of the Dueling Dragons, represented the essential false binary—the clash of opposites that are not opposites, but halves of a whole. Were Amaia and I two halves of a whole? Or were the Dueling Dragons both in me?

I wanted it to work. I wanted the work of it to earn me what I wanted. In *Heavenly Creatures*, Juliet tells Pauline: "Only the best people fight against all obstacles in pursuit of happiness." I wanted Amaia to be my happiness. *I don't make you happy*, she would say when we fought. *I can make you happy*, she would say when we made love.

An ancient alchemical text tells us, "Nature rejoices in nature; nature charms nature; nature triumphs over nature; and nature masters nature; and this is not from one nature opposing another, but through the one and same nature, through the alchemical process, with great care and great effort."

Hummingbirds hovered in her backyard, but there were no flowers, so together we filled a feeder with sugar water and watched them, those bright breasted fairies who drank so gently.

Our words had always clashed, but not our bodies. Her mouth on my breast, my belly, the hum of her between my legs, the hot nectar she pulled from me with her long fingers. Early beekeepers were called *honey-pullers*—a sensual name, though honey-pullers tore those hives with spears of wood, broke them open so the colony had to start over and build a new world from scratch. Maybe every beginning is such an apocalypse, every new world the end of the one that came before it.

Over time, even in the time before Alice, I noticed something. In a bar, in her truck or my car on the way home, Amaia would kiss my neck. She would bite my palm or slip her finger into my mouth. She would slide her hands over my breasts and between my legs. She would whisper in my ear all the things she wanted to do to me. *Wait until we get home*, she'd say.

But when we got home she would flop on the bed and stare at her phone. She would brush her teeth and crawl under the blankets. When I reached for her in the dark, she pushed me away. She crossed her arms over her chest. *Stop*, she'd say. *Why do you make everything about sex?* I would roll away from her, embarrassed.

In the morning, I would try to talk about it. *I felt confused*, I'd say. *I felt rejected.*

Sometimes, she'd say—*Well, if you really wanted me, you wouldn't have stopped. Why did you get so nervous?*

Sometimes, she'd say—*Stop it! We don't have any sex problem. You're inventing a problem for us. Why are you doing that?*

Sometimes, on our visits, this would go on for days and days. I would give up, ragged with uncertainty and desire. She accused me of confusing sex with other things, with comfort. And I did conflate the two. But I was not confused.

Our sex was the only certain thing between us, and that certainty was a comfort. When she finally reached for me, I would nearly weep with relief.

See? she'd say. *That's how it's supposed to be. Just natural.*

49

Jon and I drove away from that little town in silence. He directed me to his girlfriend's place, a single story, vinyl-sided house. A set of crumbling brick steps led to the front door, an empty soda bottle on the bottom step. As we stared from the parked car, a human shape darkened the window and disappeared, replaced by the blue flicker of a television.

My girlfriend's son, said Jon, shaking his head. *He's never had a job, just lies around the house and drinks beer. Lives off of her like he doesn't even want his own life.*

I shook my head in sympathy.

It was nearly dark, that time of day when my loneliness has always grown strongest, slipped out from under trees and cars, riding the shadows like smoke, curling under windows and doors, along the walls, into me. I wanted to go home. I wanted him to get out of my car. I was done, ready to retreat into my own shadows. I had no need to memorialize this moment, and I itched to drive away from it, from this sad house and its sad contents, from him. He just sat there, hands twitching against his thighs.

Thank you, he said, and turned. His gaze searched me. I didn't know what he wanted. Probably, after the long afternoon, he wanted a beer. Maybe he didn't want to go into that house. Maybe I looked like a way out, as my mother had looked like a way out.

This is a big step for us, he said.

I grimaced. *I'll see you later, Jon,* I said. He nodded and opened the car door. But instead of getting out, he leaned toward me and flung an arm around my shoulder to clasp me in an awkward hug. Then he climbed out and shut the door. Before walking up the driveway, he leaned down to the car window and looked at me one last time. He waved from the other side of the glass and I waved back.

I watched him cross the yard, his gait uneven, his self-conscious hands dangling at his sides. He climbed those broken stairs with knowing feet, shoulders hunched. He disappeared into the house without looking back.

It was tempting to see him as a symbol. Jon, the living embodiment of everything I feared and hated in myself. Jon, the ghost of Christmas future—a warning of what lay at the end of my own compulsions. But driving away from him, I knew none of these were right. Jon was just a man. He was a father with no children. An animal surviving the best way he knew how. I didn't need to fear him. There was nothing he could take away from me. There was nothing he could give me that wasn't already mine. I could look away, but I could not erase him, as I could not erase myself.

It rose in me before I reached the end of the street. I made myself drive out of town. At the first gas station off the highway, I pulled over, my chest already heaving. I turned up the radio and yielded to it. This time, I wasn't crying for her.

I cried for Jon. For his busted body climbing those crumbled steps. His wasted life. I cried for my mother, a child alone in that scrap of a town, trying to build a life with a broken man. I cried for old Pat, for her waking every day to fifty years of love gone. I cried for Mina, chasing and erasing her own history. I cried for Pop, who was once a Real Indian, whom life taught that it was better not to be what he was, and who listened. Who could blame him? He wanted to be the beginning, to leave centuries of breaking behind, just like those goddamn pilgrims. But it was impossible. There was no new world. And I was always coming for him.

50

There was a girl.

I remembered Cristina, whom Amaia had mentioned dining with during our separation, and I noticed when her name started appearing on Amaia's phone.

In Cristina I saw the sweet glow that tells the work of fifty thousand bees. The kind of beauty built out of desire and reliant on it. She was just the kind of girl to fall for Amaia. She was a lot like me.

The power of beauty is also a weakness. It is a circus tent propped on slender poles of desire. Most see only the spangled constellation of a girl overhead. Amaia loved a spectacle, but she saw the tent poles, how one kick could collapse the whole show. She couldn't resist.

She's pretty, I said.

Really? said Amaia. *I've never thought about it.*

Bullshit, I thought.

Amaia's phone made the sound of a wave whenever a message delivered. *Swoosh*, it crashed on the nightstand. It seemed that every time I looked at that screen, I saw Cristina's name. There is a German word—*backpfeifengesicht*—that means *a face in need of a fist*. When I heard the crash of that tiny wave as it carried her name to the surface of Amaia's screen, I pictured her pretty face and thought, *backpfeifengesicht*. I had only ever hit three people in the face who hadn't paid me to and I wanted that girl for my fourth. When I saw her name on Amaia's screen, my heart spun. My hands drenched. My face flushed.

Stop it, Amaia said, and frowned. She thought I was in no position to accuse her of anything. *You can't act like that.*

I tried to stop, but every time I heard that wave, my ears went conch shells. They filled with rushing. Some say it is the ocean we hear in conch shells, though we know that isn't true. I've heard that it is the rush of our own blood, but that's also wrong. It is the sound of the room we are in, gathered and given back to us.

You're hearing things, she said. *You're imagining it.*

With her, I was jealous. More than I had ever been. But I was not prone to imagining things. My instincts felt true.

There's something there, I said to her. *I know it.*

You're paranoid, she said. *There is nothing between us. I thought you wanted me to have more friends?*

I tried to believe her. *I must be mad*, I thought. *I hope I am mad.*

51

In the 1944 film *Gaslight*, starring Ingrid Bergman, a husband convinces his wife she is mad by manipulating minor elements in their home and projecting qualities onto her that she does not exhibit. He gifts her an heirloom brooch and then hides it from her. "You are inclined to lose things, my dear," he tells her. When she questions his suspect behavior, he asks her, "Are you becoming suspicious as well as absentminded?" As he searches for hidden jewels in their attic, the gas lights of their home dim and when his wife inquires, the husband convinces her that she imagined it. The film was advertised as "the strange drama of a captive sweetheart," and earned Bergman that year's Academy Award for Best Actress.

At a conference in Boston, I waited for Amaia in the hotel room. I opened her computer. I typed the word *Cristina* into the search window and found the e-mails in her trash folder.

Amaia had written: *I am thinking of that poem. About "the face that launch'd a thousand ships" and "burnt the topless towers of Ilium." Like the kiss in that poem, your mouth took something from me, or gave me something. I'll keep it always.*

The girl's mouth had given her something. I read all the e-mails. I watched her build a story for the girl out of the same phrases she'd used on me. The same tricks, I thought. And they were tricks. But that didn't make it hurt less.

I took a picture of the words she had written to both of us. I sent her the picture.

FUCK YOU, I wrote.

I packed my suitcase. My heart muscle contracted. Maybe, it stopped. A chamber closed. I had a heart left, but not my right heart.

I called Amit. *I'm leaving*, I said.

Are you sure? she asked.

But I didn't leave.

Amaia returned, breathless and pale. *I love you*, she said.

Fuck you, I said.

I love you, she said.

You can fuck yourself, I said. *You can fuck that girl, too. And then you can fuck her over like you did me and like you did your wife.*

She blocked the hotel room door with her body.

I love you, she said, backing me into the room. *It was so stupid. I was just scared.*

I slapped her face. She didn't even flinch.

Stay, she said.

To face your Imago and walk through it is to re-enact the most painful parts of your beginning. The point is to find or create a new ending. Most of the time we don't. But we try again.

It's an addiction, Amit told me. I typed "love addiction" into my browser window. Even the misspelled descriptions and lists of warning signs in purple font described us. How do we know when to stop trying? And what if, when that time comes, we cannot? Lessons often arrive in the form of lovers, and lessons keep us captive until we learn them. My lessons keep calling until I answer. They wait in a parked car outside the house. They are infinitely patient. In this way, every lesson is "a strange drama of a captive sweetheart." Sometimes, we need a glue so strong it is part poison.

"I am mad," Bergman laments in *Gaslight*. "I'm always losing things and hiding things and I can never find them, I don't know where I've put them." She is wrong and she is right. She has lost things and hid things, but not the ones she thinks. Not the ones her husband tells her she has lost. Not the brooch, but herself.

52

Soon after the conference in Boston, Amaia was scheduled to give a lecture. I knew Cristina would be in the audience. Before the lecture, Amaia sent me her draft for notes. The paper was excellent. In it, she wrote about Marlowe's Helen, about "the face that launch'd a thousand ships."

Please don't include that, I asked her.

It has nothing to do with her, she said. *Who cares if she thinks it does?*

Please take it out, I said.

She did not. She delivered the lecture. Cristina sat in the front row. I stood in the back. When she finished, I went to the restroom and screamed into my hands.

I need some space, I told her. I just needed a couple of weeks to gather my thoughts.

That doesn't make any sense, she said. *You're coming here in a few days.*

I canceled my ticket, I said.

She called me weeping, then accusing, then begging. She could not let me be.

I need to talk to you, she said.

I need you to give me some space, I said.

She sent me a long letter. For the first time, I did not answer.

I opened my world to you, she wrote. *I tore it apart. To you, I suppose my world is not so special. I am not so special.*

Of course, I wanted to argue with her. But I did not.

A few days before Easter, at the end of the first week, I sat at my desk. If I couldn't yet make sense of things, I could at least record them. At dinner that night, over cayenne-dusted tortilla chips and guacamole, I had told Amit that something felt different. I hurt, still, but the squall in me had begun to settle, lights to flicker. The strange sensation of seeping back into myself. My friend had looked so relieved.

That night, I was writing about my trip with Jon when I heard a soft knock at my apartment door. I pushed back my chair and walked the few steps to open it.

Amaia. A familiar sweatshirt hung on her broad shoulders, a suitcase in her hand, and her face so soft with hope that it broke me open like a street melon—the sun-soaked ones they sell on Nostrand Avenue in summer. Once, I watched one roll off the pile and hit the pavement, hot rind cracked open to the sugared center. She could have sunk a spoon into me.

I let her in. I took her suitcase and pulled her into my arms, and she folded over me, hair cold against my cheek, breath hot on my shoulder. Her neck was so sweet. It was a place I had thought of so many times. I tasted it and saw stars—Maia, Electra, Taygeta, Alcyone, Celaeno, Sterope, and my lost Merope.

When I told Amit that she had shown up, Amit looked so tired. She said, *I'm sorry. I can't do this with you anymore.* She said, *I love you. Call me when it's over.*

53

The next time I arrived in Torrington, Jon and Pat greeted me in the kitchen, freshly dressed and smelling of soap. They were ready to go. Joan sat at the table, elbow propped on her Bible, a cigarette between her fingers dribbling smoke toward the cracked window.

Aren't you coming? I asked. *Oh, no, I'm tired and you know, my breathing is bad today,* she said, though I could tell she wanted to join us. *It'll be time for you to spend alone with Jon,* she added. I understood that he had asked her to stay behind.

I led Pat to the passenger-side door and Jon stopped me. *Oh, no, she can sit in the back,* he said. He wanted to sit in the front with me. I had always craved being wanted, but there is a principle difference between wanting someone and wanting someone to give you something. I had wished to be possessed, but not excavated. I knew the addict's heat vision—how it turns people into blurs of body warmth, the red glow of what you want from them the only vivid thing.

An early drug experience: my first girlfriend and I decided to try magic mushrooms. Something flipped in me. When we encountered hiccups in our quest to find them, she didn't care much. She was distracted, ready to return to our usual pastimes of kissing and crying. In the months I had known her, I had thought of nothing but her. Until that day. Suddenly, I wanted her to shut up. I wanted her to stop touching me and help me find those drugs. *Who cares?* she said. *We'll do it another time. You're scaring me*, she said. My heat vision had turned from her and she felt the sudden cool of it. I was gone. She hadn't known I could disappear like that.

We like to call it Oz, Jon said of the casino. He wanted something from me, and he wanted me to drive him to that Emerald City. Maybe that was all he wanted on that sunny afternoon. It took two hours to drive there. Jon reached his hand into the back and tugged on Pat's cane. She cackled with delight at what was clearly a favorite game.

Did you see my new scooter? Jon asked me. I had, in the driveway of Joan's house. *Spiffy*, I said. *How'd you score that?*

With Pat's money, he said, hackles risen.

I said nothing.

I take care of her, he said. *People get paid a lot to do what I do for her.*

54

Amaia and I drove to the Cape. We drove in the dark and laughed all the way. She was doing everything right and still it didn't calm the nervous churn in me, the voice that said your true love should not be anathema to everything else good in your life, should not turn you into a desperate stranger, a person unable to say no. But still, I wanted her.

As we crossed the Massachusetts state line, I spotted a hair salon—Hairy Situations. *Reminds me of a place upstate*, I said. *Hair's the Deal!* We were glad to laugh, mouths salty from truck stop snacks.

Vanity Hair, she said.

Fresh Hair with Terry Gross, I countered.

The Canterbury Hairs.

Hair ships of purple gently toss.

But thy eternal summer shall not fade,

Nor lose possession of that hair thou ow'st;

Hairy Tales to Tell in the Dark.

Hair Supply.

I laughed so hard that I begged her to stop. I was going to piss my pants and we were on a long wooded stretch of highway with no exit in sight.

Goldilocks and the Three Hairs.

Grimm's Hairy Tales.

The Hair Up There.

Hair! The Herald Angels Sing.

The Hair in the Moon.

In one version, "The Hare in the Moon" is a story of a selfless rabbit who offers his own flesh to feed his hungry companion. As a reward, he is placed in the moon as an example to all of true selflessness. The entry of Borges's *Book of Imaginary Beings* dedicated to "The Hare in the Moon," however, recalls the last lines of Canto XX in Dante's *Inferno*: "Cain with his thorn-bush [striding] the sill / Of the two hemispheres." After he murders Abel, Cain is imprisoned in the moon by the Lord. There, he carries a bundle of thorns for eternity. Our stories tell us that some passions are rewarded and others punished. But passion always feels justified. Everyone is a Hare in their own mind, even Cain. In our passion, we rarely know if it will lead to salvation or damnation. And sometimes, it is both.

In Canto XX, Dante finds a procession of sinners with their heads turned backward. Horrified at these head-spun wretches, he weeps and is chastised by Virgil. The final reference to Cain with his thorns means only that the moon is low and the aggrieved hero is ready to move on.

A few weeks before our vacation, I drove to visit my brother in his communal household in Northhampton, Massachusetts. I spent the drive chewing on my own mind, and most of the day telling him about my own troubles: my ambivalence about our love, the way we couldn't stop hurting one another. He offered little advice, but listened well, and by the time we started dinner, I felt easier, less bound by my own obsession.

On the wall of my brother's bedroom was a printed quote from the German psychotherapist and Zen master, Karlfried Graf Dürckheim: "The man who falls upon hard times . . . will seek out someone who will faithfully and inexorably help him to risk himself, so that he may endure the suffering and pass courageously through it, thus making of it a 'raft that leads to the far shore.'" I tossed alone in his creaky loft bed that night, wondering how you knew when you reached the far shore. And what you did when you got there.

A few days before our vacation, I had lunch with a former teacher of mine—now mentor and friend. I told him our story. I wanted him to tell me what to do. Or that I had done the right thing by staying.

Marriage, he said, *is a list of grievances. Among other things.* I had my thorn bush, he meant. As she did. As we all do, if we stay long enough.

I wanted to ask him if my head was on backward. There were the grievances, yes. I could forgive her, or I could leave. But what of the constant itch in me? What about the part of me that felt, without any drama or fanfare, that the choice was not to stay or to go. The choice was her or me.

55

The Mashantucket Pequot are part of the diaspora of Algonquin-speaking indigenous people that include the Wampanoag, Narragansett, and Delaware. The Pequot reservation was created by the Connecticut Colony in 1666, after the tribe had been nearly annihilated.

In 1677, the Puritan colonist William Hubbard postulated that predating the pilgrim's landing, the Pequot had moved coastward from points in the Hudson Valley. He depicted them as invaders from "the interior of the continent" who "by force seized upon one of the places near the sea, and became a Terror to all their Neighbors." The irony of this perception, like so many in the history of colonization, cannot be overstated.

When the last tribal member living on the Pequot reservation, Elizabeth George, died in 1973, the federal government initiated the process of reclaiming the tribal land. In 1983, after a ten-year fight for federal recognition, Ronald Reagan signed the Connecticut Indian Land Claims Settlement Act, which included recognition of the Mashantucket Pequot.

Now, the Pequot reservation land is home to Foxwood's— the largest casino in the United States and Jon's favorite place to gamble.

Frank L. Baum built the Emerald City out of his own nightmares. As a boy, he suffered recurrent dreams of a scarecrow whose "ragged hay fingers" grasped for his neck. His fear of struck matches came after a theater burned during a production of his play, *Matches*. Baum's mother-in-law had conducted research on witch-hunting whose horrors engraved his imagination. In *The Wonderful Wizard of Oz*, whose film adaptation my abuela often played for my brother and me, Baum wanted the magic of Grimm's fairy tales without their horror. In his book's introduction, he states that "it aspires to being a modernized fairy tale, in which the wonderment and joy are retained and the heart-aches and nightmares are left out." And likewise, he reversed the power of his own fears. His scarecrow becomes a jester. His witch deserves her morbid fate.

Years before he penned *The Wonderful Wizard of Oz*, Baum wrote an editorial for a newspaper in South Dakota in response to the death of Sitting Bull and the massacre at Wounded Knee. In it he called for the killing of all remaining Indians. "Why not annihilation?" he asked. "Their glory has fled, their spirit broken, their manhood effaced; better that they die than live the miserable wretches that they are." Even when the "heart-aches and nightmares" that troubled him were living people, he wanted them eradicated. Self-protection can be that merciless.

The people of the Emerald City wear green goggles to believe that their city is made of emeralds. Ten years before the book's release, Baum published a story about a farmer in a drought who dresses his horse in green goggles to trick the horse into believing that the wood chips he feeds on are grass.

Green goggles, heat vision, cathected attachment—we all build our Emerald City. Out of people, slot machines, sparkling powders, and smoke. I saw Jon's eyes shine as we drove into the casino parking lot. *You'll never win*, I wanted to tell him. But who was I to call his salvation a damnation? It was both, of course.

Amaia and I wandered the narrow sidewalks of Provincetown, happily invisible amidst the stream of gay men and tourists. We bathed nude on the sundeck of our hotel and ate the same mediocre, overpriced meal at every restaurant in town. And my phone didn't ring. No one but my mother even knew we were on vacation.

We made love—my bite less ravenous than it had ever been. And we did not fight. We climbed to the top of Pilgrim Monument and looked out over the bay as the wind lifted my skirt. The water and the sky folded us in its envelope of cool color, damp with salted mist.

By the time the *Mayflower* landed in Provincetown in 1620, five weeks before Plymouth Rock, two thirds of the Wampanoag Nation had already been killed by disease. French explorer Samuel de Champlain led a mapping expedition in 1605, landing precisely where the Plymouth Colony would later settle. For nearly one hundred years prior, European fur traders had made excursions on the coast between Maine and Massachusetts, delivering yellow fever, smallpox, spotted fever, and typhoid.

When I stood on the shore of Plymouth Beach as a child and imagined the sight of that ship, I had imagined it a wonder. Maybe the Wampanoag did wonder, but they also probably recognized their ruin. Of the 45,000 already dead, the largest numbers were of Elders and children— the surest way to lose a language. They didn't know what to call the white devils, but they knew their words were in danger.

The 252-foot monument commemorates the Pilgrims' first landing and the signing of the Mayflower Compact, which states: "Having undertaken, for the glory of God, and advancement of the Christian faith, and honor of our King and Country, a voyage to plant the first colony in the northern parts of Virginia, do by these presents solemnly and mutually, in the presence of God, and one of another, covenant and combine our selves together . . . to enact, constitute, and frame such just and equal laws, ordinances, acts, consti- tutions and offices, from time to time, as shall be thought most meet and convenient for the general good of the Colony, unto which we promise all due submission and obedience."

As we climbed those 116 winding steps and sixty ramps, we passed plaques that honored the *Mayflower* descendants and founders of familiar towns. It chilled me to think of those earnest people. They believed in their god, and their good. They believed in their right to extract submission and obedience not only from themselves but from the people whose land they'd claimed. They believed in the Calvinist doctrine of predestination—that God doled salvation to some and eternal damnation to others. They believed in the genocide of these people, in their enslavement, in the trade of native men and boys—deemed too dangerous to keep in the colony—for African slaves. The first African slaveholders in this country were the Massachusetts colonists.

The pilgrims were those head-spun wretches. Maybe they also carried that thorn-bush.

In the museum at the base of the monument are a series of dioramas, beginning with "The First Encounter," in which the Wampanoag fought and then fled the interlopers, surely fearing their pestilence as much as their gunpowder. At the next, Amaia burst into laughter. The diorama featured a cast of hungry pilgrims amid neat rows of cornstalks. "Finding the Corn," read the title.

Finding the corn! We both doubled over.

More like stealing *the corn.* We laughed so hard. We laughed at that human ability to build the story we wish for, and make it true. Laughed at a wish so fervent it lived for centuries. Laughed that there was not a single diorama depicting the lives or deaths of those natives. Laughed that we still managed to be surprised by this, in the year 2014.

Until then, I had resisted the draw of that history. Maybe it was in me, but I would not colonize it with my white fetishism. How could I ever know my own motives? The Pilgrims believed God had cleared a path, that the pestilence delivered by other whites was a path the Lord had cleared for them. They called it "The Miraculous Plague." The natives called it "The Great Dying." By the time of King Philip's War—the end of the Wampanoag tribe—there were less than a thousand left to kill.

By the summer of 2014, I knew both the glory of conquer and the erasure of colonization. My own small tastes of these, and the legacy of them that built me: my European people, my native people, my captain's Taino people. At the top of that granite tower, I knew I was both head-spun sinner and Hare in the Moon. In me were both brothers, all the circles of Hell, damnation and salvation. Like Dante, I wept, and then walked back down those steps.

Later, in the hotel, Amaia knelt between my legs. She reached her hands up over my belly, my breasts, and then pulled me by the hips, pressed her tongue into me. After, we lay side by side, arms draped across each other's bodies.

You know, she said, winding my hair around her palm. *You can call yourself an Indian.* I nodded. I also knew I didn't need to. What I'd found inside me was enough.

57

We stayed at Foxwood's for two hours. Jon settled Pat into her favorite machine—the Lucky 7's—and then followed me to a game of my own choosing: Tiger Treasure slots.

Don't you have your own favorite game? I asked him.

I like watching you, he said.

I nodded. I could let him watch me. I was there to watch him, too.

I scored a bonus and digital tigers danced across the screen, accompanied by bells and whistles. I thought of Borges's *Dreamtigers*, and the hubris of thinking we can conjure our own beasts. "Oh, incompetence!" laments Borges. "Never can my dreams engender the wild beast I long for." His tiger appears, but it is stuffed. It is weak and it has the touch of a smaller animal—a bird, a dog. Maybe, a man.

I went to the ladies room and when I returned Jon had gone. I wandered the casino floors and pressed my fingertips against my arm, my thigh, my mouth. All my life, I had surveyed strangers' faces, woken to rooms I didn't know, unfathomably far from the rooms that knew me. I had felt like smoke, dissolved into particles, reassembled in some Emerald City. In that smoke-soaked place, I knew that there was no Emerald City. And I had always been.

On the drive home we laughed. Something had shifted, maybe each of us sated in our own way. Jon smelled like liquor and Pat muttered in the backseat. *What a beautiful day*, she said. *What a beautiful day.*

I cannot save these people, my people, from their addictions. Maybe I cannot even love them. But I can laugh with them. I can look at them. And I know that looking can be the truest kind of love.

For the first time, I did not cry as I drove away from them.

In a letter to Bill Wilson, the founder of Alcoholics Anonymous, Jung wrote that the hunger of addiction is "the equivalent, on a low level, of the spiritual thirst of our being for wholeness, expressed in medieval language: the union with God."

I have often thought of love in those terms. Its craving is also a hunger for wholeness. Jung's solution to addiction—*spiritus contra spiritum*—suggests that God is the only thing that can sate our craving. I know that God is in other people. But people are not gods. We can't find wholeness in them any easier than in a bottle.

These people I found are the people from whom I learned hunger. I also learned it from the people who loved me. My affliction, the thing I have tried so many times to define, to resist, to eradicate, to succumb to—it is the hunger of the abandoned. It is the result of being cut off from yourself. That hunger, denied, becomes a hunger for other things.

Every addiction, every mad love transcends the legacy of singular people. Historical trauma is a legacy of abandonment, of erasure. I believe in the science of genealogy. But I don't think science invents us—we invented it. We saw the symptoms of centuries of genocide, of lost language, of estrangement, and we called them systems. The Wampanoag people lost everything. My Taino legacy is the same legacy of the Cherokee, the Navajo, the Aztec, all of us. Call it science, how a hunger is built into a body. Call it reincarnation. Call it any word. We don't conjure our tigers. They have been dreaming us all along.

58

A few days before Amaia moved to New York, I called my mother. *I think I want to write about all of this*, I told her. *But I feel like I'm not supposed to. It's about too many things. It's not enough of any one thing.*

It's about you, she said. *Isn't it? About how you are not enough of any one thing.* It was true. I am Puerto Rican, but not really. Indian, but not really. Gay, but not really. Adopted, but not really. I cringed at the thought. I'd never wanted to be one of those people who felt not enough.

It seems like a very American story, my mother said.

It struck me that she was right.

Can I tell you something terrible? I asked.

Of course.

Sometimes, I wish Amaia would do something awful, so that I could leave her.

My mother paused before answering. *She already did, honey.*

On the first day of class, I often subject my students to an uncomfortable exercise. I ask them to turn to the person seated next to them and make direct eye contact for one minute. If there is an odd number of students, I participate in the exercise. Try not to laugh, I urge them. Try not to look away or dissociate. When my timer goes off, they collectively sigh. It is hard for them. For most people, this kind of sustained eye-contact only precedes violence or sex.

But in that minute, the room tone changes. The usual jostling of egos, of postures and fears that assume so much space, dissipates. We are all more naked, as Berger defines it in *Ways of Seeing*, "To be naked is to be oneself." That is, in looking at each other, we become less occupied with being seen. Something else enters the room. Reverence, maybe. If you want to write about something, I tell them, you have to look at it. You have to look long enough that your own reflection fades. Total self-absorption is the dubious luxury of non-writers. If you want to write about yourself, I tell them, you must meet your own gaze with this same attention.

We all craft a story we can live with. The one that makes ourselves easier to live with. This is not the one worth writing. To write your story, you must face a truer version of it. You must look at the parts that hurt, that do not flatter or comfort you. That do not spare you the trouble of knowing what made you, and what into.

I used to wonder if my own difficulty in doing this made me a hypocrite. Now, I'm not sure I believe in hypocrites. We often prescribe for others the thing we most need. It is part of how we learn.

59

I waited at baggage claim with balloons, a pizza, and flowers. Amaia walked toward me and I saw the trepidation on her face. I saw her searching for something that looked like home. I looked at the baggage carousel.

We drove over the Verrazano Bridge, the city glittering ahead. *Look*, I said. *Do you feel it?*

She looked at the constellation of lights, at my city, and then at me.

You don't want me here, she said.

Yes I do, I said.

You want to, she said. *But you don't.*

There was a fight about money. It felt so ugly. Before she had moved to New York, Amaia had asked if I would continue paying the rent on the apartment. She was keeping her house and car in the desert and was concerned about expenses. Amaia had ten times the amount of savings that I did and earned nearly twice what I did in regular salary. Still, I understood. Partly, I understood her worry as misplaced anxiety about moving her life to New York. I agreed to pay the rent until she felt more secure.

After a month, it stopped feeling all right. The lack of parity felt like a reflection of other imbalances in our relationship. Once again, I felt alone with the burden of our complete reality. Once again, I had compensated because I understood that she could not see it.

I thought hard about how to approach the subject. Asking for things from her had never gone well. I consulted my therapist on the best way. One morning, I cautiously asked her if she could contribute a third of the rent. It did not go well.

But you chose to live in this city, she said. *It's ridiculously expensive.*

And now you have chosen to live here, I said. *And to keep your other life intact.*

It doesn't even feel like my apartment, she said.

I wanted to see it her way. Our stalemate was agony. It went on for days. Finally, I agreed to keep things as they were. *It's fine*, I said. But it did not feel fine.

A week later, she was scheduled to present at a conference an hour away. As usual, she wanted me to go with her.

I can't do it, I said. *I have to get my own work done. I need to go to my meetings. I need to see my friends.*

You can get more work done there, she said. *You'll have the hotel room to yourself. You won't be distracted.*

I'll come on the second day, I bargained.

Fine, she said. But it wasn't fine.

I drove her to the conference. The hotel reeked of old smoke and the children in the next room screamed all morning. I attended Amaia's first presentation and, as always, she was wonderful. I hooted from my front row seat with pride and then we ate dinner with her colleagues.

I was desperate to accomplish something the next day. Amaia slept badly and in the morning was frantic before her second presentation.

Can you print my notes and bring them to the conference center? she asked.

What about checkout? I asked. *Don't we have to leave by noon? When will you be done?* The room was scattered in piles of clothes, shoes, and books. Toiletries littered the bathroom counters.

I'm sorry, she said.

I printed and delivered her notes, packed our suitcases, and loaded the car. After checkout, I waited for an hour in the idling car outside the conference center until she finished.

I felt petty. I hated my frustration. But it wasn't this time that mattered. It was every time. When I'd brought it up under similar circumstances, Amaia had been shocked and deeply hurt.

You're not used to working like a team, she had said. *I would do it for you*, she said. *Next time, it will be your turn.*

But if I am always helping you, I thought, then I will never get to my own work. It will never be my turn.

When I thought of Amit my heart hurt. I tried not to think of Amit. When my mother called to see how things were going,

I didn't answer. I had not called my brother in months. Amaia and I were together nearly all the time.

There were no more fights about text messages or phone calls because no one texted or called anymore. In *The Book of Hours*, Rilke writes, "I am too alone in the world, and yet not alone enough / to make every moment holy." I missed my friends. I missed myself. I even missed her. I told myself that this was everything I'd wanted. I told myself that I just needed to adjust to the change. But it didn't feel like an adjustment. It felt like I couldn't breathe.

One morning, I stood in the bathroom. Through the cracked door, I saw the slope of her leg, her elegant foot on the wood floor. I felt such an ache of tenderness for that small slice of her that I braced myself, hand against the wall.

It kept happening. Her earlobe after I removed her earring. Her hands on her thighs in the passenger seat of my car. A swirl of her hair on the bedroom floor. Her neatly folded T-shirts in a drawer. While she slept, I smelled her perfume bottle, as if she had already gone.

Sometimes you love someone most of all as you are leaving them.

I could not see her for so long. I saw only the red throb of what I wanted from her. *Love me*, I asked her. *Heal me*, I meant. In the end, I wanted my green goggles back. I wanted the infrared vision of cathexis. I didn't want the true story. I wanted my story.

A few nights after the conference, we drove home from the university where I teach. We sang with the radio, my hand on the back of her neck as she drove. She had begun trying to convince me to move to the New Jersey suburbs.

We can buy a house, she said. *You won't have to commute anymore. Think how much more writing you'll get done. Think how much money we'll save.*

It seemed almost possible. She painted such a beautiful picture. In moments, I believed in it. But then, alone with my thoughts, the fantasy dissolved. I loved my city. It wasn't the city that kept me from writing. It wasn't my friends who kept me from writing. The idea of being even more isolated from the people who knew me gave me chills.

I knew it wasn't real. Maybe, if we were different, it could have been. If there had been enough room for two in our world, maybe we could have moved it anywhere. But there wasn't. I needed her to make more space for me. I needed real parity—something we'd never had. I think she knew that she was losing me. That her only options were to change how we worked or to let me leave. She didn't want to do either of those things, so she invented a third option: this life in the suburbs, where I would have more time and money, and we could be happy. She wanted me to be happy, I know. And this way, she wouldn't have to change anything. But it was like a necklace of maggots. If I turned it this way, they looked like pearls. But they weren't pearls. It was a sacrifice wrapped as a gift.

For weeks I had woken to a sick feeling in my gut. I had woken to the thought, *I can't do this.* The next day, I said it out loud. *I can't do this.*

She was calm. She wanted to stay through the weekend.

Of course, I said.

We had dinner in a dark bar at a corner table. It was the quietest hurt we'd ever shared and the worst. Neither of us ate. On the sidewalk outside she pulled me against her. I crashed in a wave against her chest, over and over, wanting her to catch me, but she couldn't.

The morning she planned to leave, I woke at 4 A.M., her face wet against mine.

Please, she whispered.

I wrapped my arms around her. I wanted to quiet her. I was so tired.

Yes, I said. I can't do this, I thought.

That night, we ran through Fort Greene Park. At sunset, the lampposts burned yellow and leaves gathered in drifts along the stone walls. A small parade of children and parents wound slowly down the paths carrying paper bags with lit candles inside. Their soft torches glowed in a long tail and everything felt sweet and broken. Before going home, we drank tea and shared a beignet at a tiny French café on Dekalb Avenue.

I realized that I still could not resist her, despite my certainty. The next morning, while she slept, I wrote her a letter. I left the apartment.

Don't do it like this, she texted me, when she read the letter. *Come back.*

I didn't return until the following twilight. As I unlocked the door, I felt both hope and fear that she would be there.

The apartment was emptier than it had ever been. It felt like the first time I had ever been alone. I sat on the sofa and let the windows darken. I watched the shadows slip across the floor, drawing their cloth over all the places she was gone.

I hated how I had done it. But I wasn't gone. I was right there.

60

When I see my half sister again, we meet at a burger place in Burlington and sit on the patio. Mist dampens our hair and meaty white men in hiking boots talk vigorously at the next table. It is easier than the first lunch. I am easier. I have unfolded the exquisite corpse and seen my shadow half. I have cried my weight in tears and done the thing impossible. I am not looking for myself in her this time.

When I tell her that I've met Jon, her blue gaze widens. *Wow*, she says. *You're braver than me.*

I'm not brave, I tell her. *Just curious.* Though that's not true either. I know that I have less agency than the brave or curious. I am compelled. It is not the bondage of addiction but a different kind of drive, a hunger I cannot ignore. Maybe that's all bravery is: when your hunger is greater than your fear. I resist the implication that bravery is noble. I must face the things that scare me in order to survive. And survival is not noble. It is not a sacrifice of self but in service to the self.

I want my boy to know where he comes from, my sister says. *I want them all to know you. It's still a secret.* When she looks down at her plate, I see it. The shame in her own darkness. I want to tell her that darkness is not bad. It is only the place we can't see yet. The parts of us we have looked away from.

We are all the conquered and conquerors, but it is the parts we deny that rule us. Amaia is indigenous Chilean and Spanish; I am Italian, English, native, and Puerto Rican. Together we were a hundred wars and the spoils of those wars. We pass that legacy on in everything we do and everything we love. And when we heed an impulse to erase a part of ourselves, we always fail. You cannot erase yourself. You can only abandon it. But that piece doesn't die; it lives in exile. And when you love, when you become the home for someone else's heart, you are like a house with a prisoner in the cellar. Your beloved hears the thump of that cellar door. Your child worries at twilight, feels its blue shadows sliding into her, because she sees the twilight in you—the silvery dark of a secret, of a chosen forgetting. Pulling a curtain around something doesn't keep the dark out. It keeps it in.

I have always been afraid to have children. I didn't want to give them these parts of me—the hurtling hunger, the shame—but now I know there is no avoiding it. The best I can do is teach them not to fear the dark.

I don't say any of this to my sister. Instead, I tell her that I can be auntie, friend, sister, or stranger to her children. Whatever she needs. And if she ever needs it, I can be her map.

In 1970, 350 years after the Pilgrims landed, the Massachusetts Chamber of Commerce invited a Wampanoag speaker to present at their annual anniversary celebration. That Wampanoag man, Wamsutta James, wrote a speech about his people. He wrote about generosity repaid with enslavement, about the fifty years it took for the Pilgrims to erase the Wampanoag, and the three-hundred-year legacy of poverty, addiction, and discrimination that followed. His speech ended with the statement: "You the white man are celebrating an anniversary. We the Wampanoags will help you celebrate in the concept of a beginning. It was the beginning of a new life for the Pilgrims. Now, 350 years later it is a beginning of a new determination for the original American."

When planners previewed the speech, they proved what Wamsutta stated elsewhere in it, that "The white man in the presence of the Indian is still mystified by his uncanny ability to make him feel uncomfortable." They suppressed the speech, and instead Wamsutta and his supporters marched in protest of the celebration, inaugurating what is now known as the National Day of Mourning.

In 1997, state troopers and police used pepper spray on the peaceful marchers, among them children and the elderly.

On Thanksgiving of 2014, my brother and I drive to Plymouth and join the small crowd on Cole's Hill, where a statue of Massasoit overlooks Plymouth Rock. We stand in the cold and listen to Taino and Wampanoag Elders talk about the legacy of both our tribes.

Some believe that Columbus named the natives "Indians" not out of confusion as to his whereabouts, but from the Spanish expression *en Dios*, meaning "in God." As I stand on that hill with my brother, I feel the god in me. That is, I know I belong here. When the Taino Elder shouts, *As far as that rock over there? Turn that rock into a shrine for all our people!* I know she means my people. And when the Wampanoag Elder, at the end of his speech, gives a harsh call from the back of his throat—more bark than cry—and the crowd raises their fists in air, I know he is calling to me.

As a kid, I used to bury household objects in the yard. Then I'd draw maps to their locations and hide the maps. I first understood this habit to be one of secrecy: there was a darkness in me and I wanted to bury it.

Now I think of the maps. I think that I was learning how to keep track of my hidden things, so that I could find them when I was ready. Not a kitchen spoon or a doll's leg or a brooch, but myself.

To know where I come from is more than I ever imagined. Some burdens can only be measured by their relief.

62

When I say that I lost myself in love I don't mean that my lover took something from me. I betrayed myself. I mean that there was already something missing and I poured her into its place. I tried to make her more than herself. Amaia always tried to do a very hard thing the best way she knew how. To leave someone. To love someone. To abandon herself to something true. I know that she was chasing herself in me, too. And I hope that she found it.

It is true that every love is an angel of the abyss. Every lover is a destroyer. I had to be destroyed to become something else. To become more myself. But this freedom? It is worth it. It is worth everything.

If this is what it means to be abandoned, then let me be left. Abandon me.

Making darkness visible is a lonely process, but I have never done it alone. I could not have done it without many of these people. I owe them more than thanks.

To my brilliant and tireless and hilarious agent, Ethan Bassoff, who always calls me back and never suggested that I make this book anything other than what it is. To my family at Bloomsbury USA: Rachel Mannheimer and Nancy Miller—dream editors, Tara Kennedy, Marie Coolman, George Gibson, Laura Phillips, Laura Keefe, Jennifer Kelaher, and everyone whose names I don't know; and to everyone at Bloomsbury UK, especially Rebecca Thorne and Angelique Tran Van Sang.

To the MacDowell Colony, Virginia Center for Creative Arts, the Vermont Studio Center, the Barbara Deming Memorial Foundation, the Millay Colony, and the Lower Manhattan Cultural Council—all of whom gave me space and/or support during the writing of this book.

To the magazines that published earlier versions of these essays: *StoryQuarterly*, "The Book of Hours"; *Prairie Schooner*, "Call My Name"; *Salon*, "Leave Marks"; *The Kenyon Review*, "All of Me." To Lia Purpura and Maggie Nelson for choosing "Call My Name" and "The Book of Hours" respectively as contest winners. To Ariel Levy for giving special mention to "Call My Name" and "All of Me" in the Best American Essays anthology.

To my beloved friends in this life, among them the early champions of this book, my first readers, late-night dance warriors, back-seat editors, Scrabble nemeses, animal-video correspondents, car therapy companions, feminist conspirators, and fellows on the road of happy destiny: Shelly Oria, Nica Davidov, Anna deVries, John D'Agata, Hallie Goodman, Nadia Bolz-Weber, Caitlin Delohery, Jill Jarvis, Syreeta McFadden, Tara Clancy, Hafizah Geter, Emily Anderson, Shoshana Sklare, Nelly Reifler, Amy Gall, Pam Houston, Lydia Conklin, Kirstin Valdez Quade, Domenica Ruta, Cy Gage, Shante Smalls, May Conley, Janhavi Pakrashi, Peter Garner, Vijay Seshadri, Jo Ann Beard, Nick Flynn, Colin Beavan, Jillian Lauren, my Saturday ladies, Erin Stark, Liza Buzytsky, Cindy Cruz, Josh Weil, Ta-Nehisi Coates, Jessie Chaffee, Lidia Yuknavitch, Kiese Laymon, Meghan Daum, Melissa Chadburn, Amy King, Camille Rankine, Lynn Melnick, Cate Marvin, Erin Belieu, Jenn Baker, Antonia Crane, Sarah Hepola, PJ Mark, Lulu Sylbert, Sarah Dohrmann, James Marcus, Melissa Faliveno, Rachel Simon, Bret Anthony Johnston, Amber Dermont, Lacy Johnson, Joshua Wolf Shenk, Deborah Feingold, Katrina del Mar, Gregory Pardlo, Joy Harjo, Amanda Stern, Neil Gaiman, Amanda Palmer, Rebecca Keith, Michelle Campagna, and my hive: Francine Conley, Stephanie Danler, ZZ Packer, Brendan Basham, Tommy Zurhellen, Hilary Gulley.

To Jon Davis, Elissa Washuta, Ken White, Joan Kane, Santee Frazier, Sherwin Bitsui, Toni Jensen, Marie-Helene Bertino, Ramona Ausubel, Claire Vaye Watkins, Derek Palacio, Ismet Prcic, Manuel Gonzales, Chip Livingston, James Thomas Stevens, and all my colleagues and students and fellow writers at IAIA, the place where I first read aloud many of these pages.

To Michael Waters, Mihaela Moscaliuc, Josh Emmons, Alex Gilvarry, Alena Graedon, and all my colleagues at Monmouth University, who have given me and my work a safe harbor just in time to write this book.

To Amaia, who once said to me: "This is important. The idea to tell a story when you question how much of that story belongs to you, and you to it . . . It is a part of you no matter how big you think your part in it is. It was made for you. You were made from it. You will always belong to it."

To Jean: I wish everyone had a guide like you.

To my students: nothing has taught me more about writing and the precious gift of witness—you all know who you are.

To my family: I am so lucky. It is not easy to have a writer in the family and you have loved me so well. Thank you for your patience and for making everything possible for me.

You are the most extraordinary people. I love you more than I could ever write, but I will keep trying.

A note on "Labyrinths": Writing about one's own most powerful experiences often implicates the experiences of others, often those closest to the writer. The ethics of representing others' lives through the lens of my own subjectivity are complex. I am still learning how to navigate them with care and accountability. I regret that the limits of a single essay do not allow more room to show the immense scope of a subject so broad as "mental illness," or that of my brother's own story. My hope is that this essay will encourage those interested to continue reading. My brother's website is a good place to start: www.sustainabeast.com/fundamental-illness. There you will find more of this story in his words, and links to further resources.

Abandon Me
Melissa Febos

The following questions are intended to enhance your discussion of *Abandon Me*.

About this book

In *Abandon Me*, Melissa Febos, author of the acclaimed memoir *Whip Smart*, captures the human need for connection. She explores the different ways in which people are connected to others and the world around them: literature, family history, romantic relationships, parenthood, culture. Through the course of the memoir, Febos reconnects with her family and her Native American heritage, while grappling with both understanding the sea captain who raised her and an intense long-distance love affair with a woman. As Febos navigates these threads, she also investigates her own compulsions and instinct for self-erasure.

Abandon Me is a fearless memoir and a penetrating book that considers religion, psychology, and conceptions of sex, mythology, art, and popular culture through visceral prose.

For discussion

1. How does the cover introduce the novel and its themes? Think about the image and the color scheme in relation to the broader work. Did the cover affect the way you approached the book? What emotions does the cover evoke in you?
2. The memoir begins with three epigraphs—one from Carl Jung, one from D. W. Winnicott, and one from Violette Leduc. Do any of the epigraphs stand out more than the others? How do they work in tandem to introduce the novel?
3. The memoir is structured somewhat unconventionally. The first half is a few shorter essays, while the second half is "Abandon Me," which also serves as the title of the whole collection. How do the shorter essays work with/against the longer one?

4. Febos discusses a strong relationship with books in the early pages of her book. How do the references she makes inform the way she presents her life? Do they ever alienate you?

5. In what ways does Febos concentrate on the ways that people are acknowledged and designated? How do these ways of designation speak back to the relationships between people?

6. In "All of Me," Febos calls a 1947 portrait of Billie Holiday the "one [she] will wear on [her] body for the rest of [her] life" (91). This is not the only instance of Febos finding kindred spirits in other women. What do these women become symbols of for Febos? How are they a source of comfort? Do you have your own kindred spirits that you gravitate toward?

7. Throughout the book, Febos discusses where she came from. She thinks about her mother, her biological father, and the Captain (her adoptive father). In a moving moment in "Abandon Me," she discusses how the Captain would take her to her tribe's powwow grounds so that she could connect with her culture. How do these family members mix with family history to create a complex background that Febos must navigate? How does she perform this navigating? Does she consider herself successful?

8. Febos presents an ever-changing family structure that is marked by absence as much as togetherness. How does she come to terms with the makeup of her family? As she reconnects with her family members, what concessions does she make toward them and toward herself?

9. In "Wunderkammer," Febos says, "I was not indoctrinated in an ideal of feminine dependency by my mother" (98). In what ways does Febos engage with twenty-first-century ideals of feminism? In what ways does she not? How does the book redefine feminism in its own terms?

10. In "Girl at a Window," Febos recounts a time in Egypt when her mother was groped but was unable to retaliate. Has Febos internalized anything specific about womanhood from this event? In what other ways does Febos learn about womanhood from her mother?

11. In regard to the Captain, Febos questions: "If he loved us, if he really loved us, where was he" (115)? Part of what she comes to terms with

through these stories is understanding how people show love and understanding to what capacity they can love. What conclusions does she come to?

12. At times, Febos connects her romantic connections with the relationships that she has with her two fathers. Where does this intersection lie? Map the progression of her relationships with her fathers against the events in her romantic life.

13. Many of the characters in this book struggle with fidelity. What does Febos say about fidelity? In what ways is fidelity part of love? In what ways is it separate?

14. Febos uses motifs related to water, including but not limited to tears, the sea, seafaring. List the motifs that you noticed as you read. How do they become signposts in the text? Does their meaning change through the book?

15. Much of this memoir deals with the metaphorical consumption of humans by other people. Febos and her lover battle about this often throughout this book. By the end, what has Febos learned, if anything, about the strength of the self?

Recommended reading

Her by Christa Parravani; *Fun Home* by Alison Bechdel; *Naked in the Promised Land* by Lillian Faderman; *Inferno* by Eileen Myles; *Sita* by Kate Millett; *The Argonauts* by Maggie Nelson; *The Empathy Exams* by Leslie Jamison; *Notes from No Man's Land* by Eula Biss

Melissa Febos is the author of the critically acclaimed memoir *Whip Smart*. Her work has been widely anthologized and appears in publications including the *Kenyon Review*, *Prairie Schooner*, *Glamour*, *Guernica*, *Post Road*, *Tin House*, *Salon*, the *New York Times*, the *Rumpus*, and *Goodbye to All That: Writers on Loving and Leaving New York*, and her essays have won prizes from *Prairie Schooner*, *Story Quarterly*, and the Center for Women Writers. The recipient of an M.F.A. from Sarah Lawrence College, she is currently an assistant professor of creative writing at Monmouth University and M.F.A. faculty at the Institute of American Indian Arts (IAIA), and serves on the Board of Directors of VIDA: Women in Literary Arts. The daughter of a sea captain and a psychotherapist, she was raised on Cape Cod and lives in Brooklyn.